ENDORSEMENTS

Prepare for a journey to rediscover one of God's life-building concepts—*A Rhythm of Rest!*

A message dealing with rest, especially when presented from a spiritual point of view, is better understood and embraced by the eastern cultures—something the western mind has not championed very well in generations past.

My friend Kerrick Butler endeavors to correct the unchecked issues around rest by going to battle from the Word of God and reinforcing not only the value of rest but the necessity of it.

Our culture demands more and more attention every day to be productive and stay ahead; it has reached a chronic tipping point for a shift. This energy drink, to stay alert, society parades an exhausted lifestyle as a badge of honor. However, the cost of such living will eventually steal the very essence of a person's destiny. Without change, the fruits of restless exhaustion, sleep deprivation, and this nonstop *carnally* enforced drive will not only impact our immediate life experience, but it will also greatly alter generations to come with a variety of negatives.

Kerrick offers biblical answers to this issue in the natural and from God's standpoint. As you will see in this book, there are powerful answers that line up with God's will for His creation. I like how the message translation brings out the words of Jesus on the issue.

Matthew 11:28-30 MSG: *"Are you tired? Worn out? Burned out on religion? Come to me. Get away with me and you'll recover your life. I'll show you how to take a real rest. Walk with me and work with me—watch how I do it. Learn the unforced rhythms of grace. I won't lay anything heavy or ill-fitting on you. Keep company with me and you'll learn to live freely and lightly."*

This book is built to combat exhaustion, chaos, confusion, and many other mechanisms of the devil. If you apply yourself to what Kerrick is presenting, you will find a new quality of life that was intended by God for you from the beginning!

I wholeheartedly endorse this excellent book, *Rhythm of Rest*, by my friend, Pastor Kerrick Butler. Read it, absorb it, and watch your life change!

Joseph Z
Author, Broadcaster, Prophetic Voice
JosephZ.Com

My friend and brother, Pastor Kerrick Butler, is a voice for our times! The peace of God comes when we learn how to rest in Him. This book is a practical and scriptural call to enter into the rest that can only come from God. Kerrick tells us, "We cannot have long-life beliefs with short-life habits." This book will help us shift so that our focus and habits as believers will match the length and quality of life that we are believing for! In these busy and chaotic times, *Rhythm of Rest* is a God-sent balm for all of us!

Dr. James Tan
James Tan Ministries
International Author, *Releasing the Miraculous* and *Releasing the Anointing*

Kerrick has consistently demonstrated a deep understanding of the importance of rest, leading to a balanced and fulfilling life. *Rhythm of Rest* is an impressive, comprehensive work that reflects his profound biblical insights and personal experience. If you've ever fallen into the trap of valuing productivity at the expense of your wellbeing, this book is a path to liberation, guiding you from relying solely on your own efforts to fully trusting in God. Kerrick has truly identified the missing element for believers who seek to live the blessed life.

David S. Winston
Author, Pastor of Living Word Christian Center

After nearly three decades in full-time ministry, I've intimately experienced the relentless demands that often lead to burnout—a state that serves neither our wellbeing nor our divine purpose. Kerrick's *Rhythm of Rest* profoundly addresses this struggle, offering a compassionate guide for those in ministry, business leaders, and full-time parents alike. He illuminates how embracing God's blueprint for rest is not a luxury but a necessity for a fulfilling and impactful life. This book is a timely reminder that true fulfillment and impactful living flow from honoring the rhythm of rest God has lovingly crafted for each of us.

Mondo De La Vega, Evangelist
Bestselling Author of *My Crazy Life*
Host of *The Mondo Show*

Rest is so underrated. So many have made terrible, life-altering decisions because of a lack of it. Others have come upon amazing world-changing ideas on the heels of it. In his book, *Rhythm of Rest*, Pastor Kerrick does a phenomenal job not only explaining the importance of rest but how you can incorporate rest into your life as God has always intended.

Andre Butler
Pastor of Faith Xperience Church
Detroit, Michigan

So often in life we are constantly chasing something, causing us to be human "doings" instead of human "beings." In *Rhythm of Rest*, Kerrick Butler teaches you how to break the cycle of chasing and step into a fruitful and fulfilling life.

Tim Storey

Author, Speaker, Life Strategist, Counselor

Storey Dreams Foundation

I am thrilled to endorse my friend, Kerrick Butler, and his new book on rest! Kerrick is a long-time friend whom I've known for 20 years, and I can honestly say that he lives the message of this book. He has mastered the art of living an unhurried, unrushed, unpanicked life of faith. I have watched him weather many seasons of turbulence with the peace of God as his guide. It is with that lived experience that he has penned a book designed to be an answer for a generation plagued by anxiety and paranoia.

Kerrick takes a deep dive into the concept of experiencing the rest of God that reminds us that life doesn't have to be a constant, unsettling hustle. This book is not just for those who are feeling burnt out. It's for anyone who wants to enrich their lives with the refreshing presence of God. If you're ready to exchange your unrest for His rest, this book is for you. I can't recommend this book enough. Grab a copy and discover the transforming power of God's *rest!*

Marcus Tankard
Author of *Journey Into His Presence*
Bible Teacher, Prayer Leader

If you think you don't have time to rest or have a difficult time resting, this book is for you. You can choose to find the rhythm of rest, or you can be forced to rest. It is a choice, and Pastor Kerrick will lead you in understanding what rest is and what rest is not, and the importance of this rarely discussed topic. Come. Find a quiet place to soak up these words. Learn of the Father, learn about yourself, and learn to find the gift of rest. When you do, you will be more productive, discover more clarity, and enjoy life more. Pastor Kerrick gives you practical steps to finding rest, along with prayers to draw closer to the Father. In today's world of go, go, go, this is a must-read!

Lynn Copeland
Author/Speaker, *Prayers That Avail Much*

Let me just begin by saying I really like this book! Kerrick Butler's *Rhythm of Rest* speaks to me because it's such an important subject for the longevity and the overall health of God's people! I've tackled this topic at times in my own ministry, preaching to people about the three kinds of vacations every believer needs every year: a spiritual vacation (where you can soak, learn, and get edified); a "Mickey Mouse" vacation (a fun activity or adventure); and a local vacation (staying close to home and enjoying where God has planted you). But I've just dipped my toe into the pool of revelation that Kerrick actually swam in to write this book! And now he invites all of us to dive in with him so we can learn new rhythms of grace that help us find true rest—spirit, soul, and body. "We cannot have long-life beliefs with short-life habits," Kerrick tells us. Well, amen to that.

Let's start right there and go on a journey as we read this book to learn how to discover new rhythms that fit our call, our personality, and our circumstances. Let's tap into the wisdom of the Holy Spirit so we can finish our full course with joy, with peace, and with strength!

Roberts Liardon
Author, *God's Generals* Series

This is the book you never knew you needed! In a culture today where so many seem to get their direction from their feelings rather than truth, this is a much-needed reminder that God knows what's best for us. He knows exactly what we need, even when we don't feel like we need it—rest! There's a blessing tied to rest that you can't access any other way. One line in particular struck me deeply: "We have to get into the rhythm of the Spirit if we want to enjoy the benefits the Holy Spirit has for us." I wrote that down and put it on my desk, where I see it every day as a reminder. This book is full of small but powerful shifts—simple truths and insights that, when embraced, can lead to lasting change. I highly recommend it.

RayGene Wilson
Pastor, West Coast Life Church
Murietta, California

I'm convinced that *Rhythm of Rest* is a must-read for, at the least, most of us! Rest is the free commodity that many of us refuse to cash in. The need for rest was ordained by Elohim from the beginning of mankind's existence and yet we refuse to obey. While we label it everything from unnecessary, unimportant, impossible, or unproductive, the truth is, we are laying down a gift from the Lord.

I fell into the trap of "I'll rest when" as Kerrick talks about. When I realized that I was actually trying to earn my rest, I began to seek out the answers to change my life from living for rest to resting to live. This word that Kerrick brings will birth the understanding that rest is not only God's will, but a command given in Holy Scripture. I believe it will birth the desire, determination, and strategies to actually change our ways and find Holy Rest.

Kellie Copeland
Author, Speaker, Host of *The Kellie Show*

FOREWORDS BY
GEORGE PEARSONS & DAVID CRANK

RHYTHM
OF REST

GOD'S BLUEPRINT
FOR A FULFILLING LIFE

KERRICK
BUTLER

Published by Harrison House Publishers
Shippensburg, PA 17257

ISBN 13 TP: 978-1-6675-1142-9
ISBN 13 eBook: 978-1-6675-1143-6

For Worldwide Distribution, Printed in the U.S.A.
1 2 3 4 5 6 7 8 / 29 28 27 26 25

CONTENTS

CONTENTS

FOREWORD BY DAVID CRANK

Think about it. When was the last time you truly rested? (C'mon, passing out on the couch with the remote in hand and Cheeto dust in your hair doesn't really count.) I'm talking about deep, soul-soothing, peace-filled rest that leaves you feeling like a human being again.

Still thinking?

If you're anything like me, rest is one of those things you definitely mean to do—someday. Maybe after this week is over, or once this big project wraps up.

Spoiler alert: Every day, that day just keeps moving further and further away.

That's why this book should be required reading for the benefit of your sanity and your soul!

Kerrick Butler has written something you probably didn't even know you needed but will be incredibly grateful for. *Rhythm of Rest* is not a guilt trip. It's not a "you can do better" sermon in book form. And it definitely doesn't try to boost your productivity by suggesting you check your email while on the beach. His book is an invitation to pause. To breathe. To actually enjoy the life God gave you—not just endure it. Let Kerrick gently (and sometimes not so gently) remind you that rest isn't just a nice idea for when you retire. It's part of God's divine design. In fact, it was God's idea in the first place. He literally took an entire day off in Genesis! (Even Ferris Bueller would approve. Lol.)

I appreciate that he doesn't just lob Scriptures at us like "holy hand grenades." He walks with us. He tells stories, shares stats, and makes us laugh while also making us think. You'll probably chuckle. You might even cry. But for sure, you'll definitely want to cancel a boatload of unnecessary meetings!

This book is a must-read for burned-out parents, stressed-out students, and overworked entrepreneurs.

Even church folk, like me, who are convinced that rest is something only heathens do on Sundays. *Rhythm of Rest* will challenge your thinking and remind you what it feels like to be fully human again.

So, silence those notifications and get comfortable.

You're about to learn the sacred art of doing less and living *more!* Not by being lazy—but by being perfectly aligned with the God who knows that rest isn't the enemy of your purpose. It's your rocket fuel!

David Crank
Lead Pastor of FaithChurch.com

FOREWORD BY GEORGE PEARSONS

✌

"I REPENT!"

Well, that's a funny way to begin a foreword. Allow me to explain.

Pastor Kerrick sent me the manuscript for his book a while ago. Here is what he wrote in his cover letter to my assistant. "After speaking in chapel last year, Pastor George and I discussed the message I preached about called 'The Rhythm of Rest.' I told him that I was considering writing a book on the topic. He encouraged me to do so quickly."

He closed the letter by writing, "*I know he is really busy*, but I would be honored if Pastor George would be willing to write one of the forewords for this book."

I am embarrassed to say that I kept his manuscript on my desk for over two months. There it sat on the stack. It was crying out, "Read me! Read me!" Kerrick was absolutely right. I WAS too busy. So, I carved out a slice of time from my busy schedule and read the book.

The more I read, the more convicted I became. I realized very quickly that I was guilty of not doing what he was writing about. I wasn't taking the time to rest. I so appreciate the research, the scriptures, and the heart with which he wrote this book. It is a handbook—a manual to help us keep a balance in our lives. He is really on to something extremely important for us all. He cares deeply about the condition of the Body of Christ and what it takes to walk in a place of peace and rest.

It is my desire that as you read the book, you too will repent and become as convicted as I was to enter into a much deeper realm of God's gift to mankind: the rhythm of rest.

Pastor George Pearsons
Eagle Mountain International Church
Fort Worth, Texas

INTRODUCTION

You are called by God. Yes, you! God has a wonderful plan for your life. His plan for your life is not automatic; you have a part to play. God has His part; you have your part. There is work that you are called to do and there are paths you are called to take.

Ephesians 2:10 (AMPC) says:

For we are God's [own] handiwork (His workmanship), recreated in Christ Jesus, [born anew] that we may do those good works which God predestined (planned beforehand) for us [taking paths which He prepared ahead of time], that we should walk in them [living the good life which He prearranged and made ready for us to live].

God has a blueprint for your life. He has made plans for your life. When you're considering the plan of God for your life and all the work that you have to put in, remember that when God planned your life and issued your call, He also planned rest.

Rest is not a bad thing. Rest is not laziness. Rest is not weakness. However, many people are terrible at resting and do not know how to rest. Some people try to laugh it off and say, "Well, I'll rest when I'm dead." Sadly, their lack of rest is hastening the day of their death.

Among American adults, 14.5 percent have trouble falling asleep and 17.8 percent have trouble staying asleep.[1] Almost 40 percent of adults report accidentally falling asleep during the day, and between 50 to 70 million Americans suffer from a chronic sleep disorder.[2] Sleep deficiency can cause many health problems. "Heart disease, kidney disease, high blood pressure, diabetes, stroke, obesity, and depression" are all issues linked to sleep deficiency.[3] In fact, lack of sleep is costing the economy of the United States up to $411 billion dollars annually through lower productivity levels and a higher risk of mortality.[4] Increasing nightly sleep from under six hours to the average recommended amount of seven to eight hours could add over $226 billion dollars to the American economy per year.[5]

Did you know that over half of all Americans do not use all of their paid time off? Nearly three-fifths of American workers and over 50 percent of managers are experiencing the damaging symptoms of burnout.[6] Burnout impacts your mental capacity and function. The cognitive impacts of burnout include mental fatigue, difficulty concentrating, impaired problem solving, and forgetfulness. The economic cost of burnout is between $125 billion and $190 billion dollars annually.[7]

Too many people are working themselves almost to death. They try to take a vacation and still do not get any rest. What do some of them to do? They give up on trying to rest. Is that where you are today?

Are you a person who says, "Well, I'm just going to work hard for these decades and as soon as the kids are out of the house, I'm going to enjoy my life."

Or do you say, "One day, when this happens, I'll rest. One day, when that happens, I'll enjoy my life."

Do you know what I've noticed in the lives of people who live that way? "One day" never comes. There is always another reason not to rest or enjoy their lives. They live perpetually in the "one day when" cycle. One day when, one day when, one day when. In this book, I want to help you go from living a life of one day W-H-E-N to celebrate a life of one day W-I-Ns. As you shift to a "one day win" mentality, you will be able to learn how to rest and enter into the rhythm of rest for your life.

A one day win is simply an accomplishment, improvement, or achievement in your life. A small step into the rhythm of rest and taking advantage of an opportunity to rest is a one day win as well. As you pause, ask yourself the following questions: "What was my win today? What did I accomplish today? What did I improve today? How did I rest today?" Write your answers in your journal. As you look back, you will realize you are accomplishing and progressing more than you previously thought. One day wins, no matter how small, are worth thanking God for and celebrating. One days wins stacked upon one days wins lead to entire life transformation.

This is something that everyone should learn. Don't put this book down and say, "Well, I'll wait till the perfect time to do it. I have a lot of stuff going on."

No, no, no! The perfect time is now and we all have a lot of stuff going on. This is not something you want to put off until a later date. This is a crucial way of life that you need to embrace today and take steps toward living. I believe that if you enter the rhythm of rest, your sleep will improve, your quality of life will improve, you will recover from effects of burnout, you will enjoy life, and you will fulfill God's plan for you. If you don't get this down, you won't fulfill the plan of God for your life.

I'll prove it to you. I believe God's Word holds important truths and keys that will transform your life and help your live in the rhythm of rest. As we explore the Scriptures together, you will see that

God has rest for you. In this book, I want to encourage you to go on a journey with me that will result in a life that is better than what you have previously imagined.

CHAPTER 1

THE SABBATH

Observe the Sabbath day by keeping it holy, as the Lord your God has commanded you. You have six days each week for your ordinary work, but the seventh day is a Sabbath day of rest dedicated to the Lord your God. On that day no one in your household may do any work. This includes you, your sons and daughters, your male and female servants, your oxen and donkeys and other livestock, and any foreigners living among you. All your male and female servants must rest as you do. Remember that you were once slaves in Egypt, but the Lord your God brought you out with his strong hand and powerful arm. That is why the Lord your God has commanded you to rest on the Sabbath day.

—Deuteronomy 5:12–15 (NLT)

Why did God command the Jewish people to rest on the Sabbath? He told them that every week they were to take one day off, as a part of the covenant He made with them—a binding agreement between Him and His people. The Sabbath day was connected to that covenant. Why did he command them to observe the Sabbath? It's not a trick question. He did it because He brought them out of Egypt.

> Therefore the children of Israel shall keep the Sabbath, to observe the Sabbath throughout their generations as a perpetual *covenant*. It is a sign between Me and the children of Israel forever; for in six days the Lord made the heavens and the earth, and on the seventh day He rested and was refreshed.
>
> —Exodus 31:16–17 (NKJV)

The Sabbath day was part of Israel's covenant with God—the sign of their covenant. What is a sign of a covenant? It is a physical or symbolic token that represents the binding agreement made between two parties. They were to follow the example of God when He created the world. He worked for six days and on the seventh day He rested and was refreshed. That Sabbath day was a sign of their covenant:

Moreover I also gave them My Sabbaths, to be a sign between them and Me, that they might know that I am the Lord who sanctifies them.

—Ezekiel 20:12 (NKJV)

SABBATH LIFESTYLE

Now, when you think about the Sabbath, some people think just about one day a week, but the Sabbath was more than just one day a week. The Sabbath also referred to certain years:

While Moses was on Mount Sinai, the Lord said to him, "Give the following instructions to the people of Israel. When you have entered the land I am giving you, the land itself must observe a Sabbath rest before the Lord every seventh year. For six years you may plant your fields and prune your vineyards and harvest your crops, but during the seventh year the land must have a Sabbath year of complete rest. It is the Lord's Sabbath. Do not plant your fields or prune your vineyards during that year. And don't store away the crops that grow on their own or gather the grapes from your unpruned vines. The land must have a year of complete rest. But you may eat whatever the land produces on its own during its Sabbath. This applies to you, your male and female servants, your hired workers, and the temporary residents who live with you. Your livestock and the wild animals in your land will also be allowed to eat what the land produces."

—Leviticus 25:1–7 (NLT)

As the passage explains, the Sabbath was not only one day of the week. The Sabbath was also a year they weren't allowed to work the land. Notice what the Lord told Moses next:

If you want to live securely in the land, follow my decrees and obey my regulations. Then the land will yield large crops, and you will eat your fill and live securely in it. But you might ask, "What will we eat during the seventh year, since we are not allowed to plant or harvest crops that year?"

—Leviticus 25:18–20 (NLT)

That is a great question, right? That is a logical question. If you were a farmer, without access to a grocery store, isn't that a question you would ask? "Um, sir, what are we going to eat for the entire year?" Notice what God told them!

Be assured that I will send my blessing for you in the sixth year, so the land will produce a crop large enough for three years. When you plant your fields in the eighth year, you will still be eating from the large crop of the sixth year. In fact, you will still be eating from that large crop when the new crop is harvested in the ninth year.

—Leviticus 25:21–22 (NLT)

That is a wonderful covenant promise God made available for them! He declared that He would send His blessing upon their work and land in the sixth year. What is His blessing? The blessing of the Lord is His power that causes an individual to thrive, increase, improve, and prosper. However, we know from studying the Bible that Israel did not keep their covenant with God. They did not keep their side of the agreement. They stopped following God's ways and His laws. Of course, there are not just 10 commandments; there are 613 commands, rules, and regulations. Some of them, especially the land ones we just read, only apply to those living in the land. Some are much broader in everyday realization and fulfillment.

FORCED REST

When they stopped following God, what happened? They stopped keeping the Sabbath. Not only did they stop keeping the Sabbath, they stopped keeping the Sabbath year. God told them that if they would follow His ways, they would live securely in the land; however, if they did not follow Him, the land would kick them out. What was the result of their disobedience? They were exiled for 70 years. Why 70 years?

> So the message of the Lord spoken through Jeremiah was fulfilled. The land finally enjoyed its Sabbath rest, lying desolate until the seventy years were fulfilled, just as the prophet had said.
> —2 Chronicles 36:21 (NLT)

When they did not believe God or follow Him, they didn't let the land rest. As a result, the land entered a forced rest of 70 years. The people of God could not come back until the forced rest was over.

What is your body made out of? Where did your body come from? Genesis 2:7 (NKJV) says, "And the Lord God formed man of the dust of the ground, and breathed into his nostrils the breath of life; and man became a living being." You're made of dirt. The ground. Yes, as we learn from Genesis and throughout the Bible, you are a spirit being, but your physical body came from the earth. And should Jesus tarry, when your time is done, your body is going back to the earth.

The earth needed a Sabbath, and when it didn't get a Sabbath it entered into a forced rest. I wonder if you are dealing with symptoms of sickness, disease, and burnout in your body because you do not rest. As a result, if you cannot do what you want to do, it means your physical body is limited. In other words, you are under a forced rest because you do not rest.

Is your body enduring a forced rest right now? I think I have your attention. A forced rest is more than just burnout. Burning out is bad, but you can consider a forced rest as a far more serious and extreme case of burnout. A forced rest will prevent you from fulfilling God's plan for your life. A forced rest limits your effectiveness, will have an impact on your overall health, and will take precious time to recover from.

Let's go to Matthew 12, now that I have your attention. You might ask, "Do I need to go back to the Law and observe the Sabbath day?" No, I did not say that! Look at Matthew 12:

At about that time Jesus was walking through some grainfields on the Sabbath. His disciples were hungry, so they began breaking off some heads of grain and eating them. But some Pharisees saw them do it and protested, "Look, your disciples are breaking the law by harvesting grain on the Sabbath."

Jesus said to them, "Haven't you read in the Scriptures what David did when he and his companions were hungry? He went into the house of God, and he and his companions broke the law by eating the sacred loaves of bread that only the priests are allowed to eat. And haven't you read in the law of Moses that the priests on duty in the Temple may work on the Sabbath? I tell you, there is one here who is even greater than the Temple! But you would not have condemned my innocent disciples if you knew the meaning of this Scripture: 'I

want you to show mercy, not offer sacrifices.'
For the Son of Man is Lord, even over the
Sabbath!'"

—Matthew 12:1–8 (NLT)

The majority of the Pharisees of that day were
exceptional at keeping the letter of the law, but not
the spirit of the law. The disciples were on assignment
with Jesus. They were walking through the field with
Him, going to where Jesus was supposed to go. As
they went, they got hungry. They did not pull out
tools and begin harvesting. They simply took some
grain off the stalks and ate it. That is not what the
Law intended to forbid.

The Pharisees were looking for a way to condemn Jesus. In the parallel passage of Mark 2:27,
Jesus told this same group of Pharisees that the Sabbath was made to meet the needs of the people, and
people were not made to meet the requirements of
the Sabbath.

The Pharisees had an opposite way of thinking.
They were thinking that they were made to keep the

Sabbath. Jesus flipped the mentality when He said, "No, no, no, the Sabbath was made to keep *you*."

You weren't made to meet the needs of the Sabbath. The Sabbath was made to meet your needs. When we think about what keeping the Sabbath should look like for us, we should not keep it like the Pharisees kept it. Under the new covenant, we don't have a commanded day of Sabbath. We have a Lord of the Sabbath.

Then Jesus went over to their synagogue, where he noticed a man with a deformed hand. The Pharisees asked Jesus, "Does the law permit a person to work by healing on the Sabbath?" (They were hoping he would say yes, so they could bring charges against him.)

And he answered, "If you had a sheep that fell into a well on the Sabbath, wouldn't you work to pull it out? Of course you would. And how much more valuable is a person than a sheep! Yes, the law permits a person to do good on the Sabbath."

Then he said to the man, "Hold out your hand." So the man held out his hand, and it was restored, just like the other one! Then the Pharisees called a meeting to plot how to kill Jesus.

—Matthew 12:9–14 (NLT)

As I will share in this book, He has a way for you to fulfill His plan for your life, a way for you to rest, and a way for you to enjoy your life. We have to follow the example of our Savior, the Lord of the Sabbath.

BETTER COVENANT, BETTER REST!

Everything that I have previously shared with you is under the old covenant. As a Christian, you don't need to live by the old covenant. You can get wisdom from that covenant and understand a lot of those things, but that is not your covenant. You should read the Old Testament and the old covenant, but if you're going to rightly divide the word of truth, you have to understand which covenant is yours to live by.

Hebrews 8:6 says that we have a better covenant than the old covenant. Why is a $20 bill better than a $10 bill? For one thing, it's worth more. The 20 includes the 10, plus some more. Your new covenant has all the blessings of the old plus all the blessings of the new, and it's kept by faith.

Did you catch that? This new covenant is kept by faith. Could it be that you don't rest the way you should because of a lack of faith? The Israelites stopped keeping their Sabbath because they didn't keep their faith in God. Are you doing the same?

As we dig into the subject of biblical Sabbath, people often ask, "Do we have to worship on Saturday?" (By the way, the Sabbath under the Law began on Friday at sunset.)

No. First of all, that's not your covenant. But if you want to worship on Saturdays, have fun. Worship as much as you like on the Sabbath, but remember that you are not held to it as a rule.

The reason why churches gather on Sunday is in honor of the Resurrection of Jesus. This isn't anything new. We have been doing this since Jesus rose from the dead. It is shown throughout all of the New Testament.

As we dig into the concept and principle of the covenants, I don't want you to be confused about this issue. Notice what the following passages share with us.

> Who are you to condemn someone else's servants? Their own master will judge whether they stand or fall. And with the Lord's help, they will stand and receive his approval.
>
> In the same way, some think one day is more holy than another day, while others think every day is alike. You should each be fully convinced that whichever day you choose is acceptable. Those who worship the Lord on a special day do it to honor him. Those who eat any kind of food do so to honor the Lord, since they give thanks to God before eating. And those who refuse to eat certain foods also want to please the Lord and give thanks to God.
>
> —Romans 14:4-6 (NLT)

So now that you know God (or should I say, now that God knows you), why do you want to go back again and become slaves once more to the weak and useless spiritual principles of this world? You are trying to earn favor with God by observing certain days or months or seasons or years.

—Galatians 4:9–10 (NLT)

So don't let anyone condemn you for what you eat or drink, or for not celebrating certain holy days or new moon ceremonies or Sabbaths. For these rules are only shadows of the reality yet to come. And Christ himself is that reality.

—Colossians 2:16–17 (NLT)

Now, the old covenant still exists. The Book of Hebrews says it's ready to disappear, but it doesn't say it has already disappeared (Hebrews 8:13). That's why people can still get some benefit from living by the old covenant, but they also have access to the new covenant, too.

Under the new covenant, you are not required to only worship on the Sabbath. But for those who are still convinced that you must worship on the Sabbath, what did Paul tell you to do? Enjoy yourself. Do it because you honor God. But don't you judge somebody else because they worship on Sunday.

The practice of the Sabbath for us is different from what we see under the old covenant. But the principle of biblical rest is the same in both covenants. In the next chapter, let's circle back to the important question about rest. Is your lack of rest a sign of a lack of faith?

REFLECTION QUESTIONS

Take some time to reflect on this chapter and answer the following questions in your journal.

1. What was the sign of the old covenant?
2. Are you required to keep the Sabbath day?
3. Have you ever experienced a "forced rest"? How long did it take for you to recover from that burnout?

4. What stuck out to you the most in this chapter?

5. How will you apply what you learned in this chapter to your everyday life?

A PRAYER FOR YOU TO PRAY

Father, as I study the subject of the rest You have for me, I pray that You open my eyes and my ears to the truth of this subject. Help me to correctly analyze how I am living and make the necessary adjustments so that I can experience Your rest for my life. Thank You for helping me. In Jesus' Name, amen!

CHAPTER 2

REST: GOD'S ORIGINAL PLAN FOR MANKIND

⮂

Therefore the children of Israel shall keep the Sabbath, to observe the Sabbath throughout their generations as a perpetual covenant. It is a sign between Me and the children of Israel forever; for in six days the Lord made the heavens and the earth, and on the seventh day He rested and was refreshed.

—Exodus 31:16–17 (NKJV)

We have to get into a rhythm of life that is led and conducted by the Holy Spirit. In His rhythm, there's time to work at a fast pace, there's time to work at a slow pace, and there's time to rest and pause. We have to get into the rhythm of the Spirit if we want to enjoy the benefits the Holy Spirit has for us.

Under the old covenant, the Sabbath day was a sign. They were to work six days and rest the seventh. That rest day, the Sabbath, was called holy. It was so holy, it was called a sign.

You being able to rest is now a sign of your new covenant. When you make the declaration that you will work six days and rest one day, you're saying, "I have so much faith in God that God will cause my six days to be more productive than my seven days." It's similar to the concept of tithing. When I tithe, it is a declaration of faith that I believe that I can do more with 90 percent of my income plus the blessing of God than I can do with 100 percent of my income on my own.

When we take the path of resting as the Spirit of grace leads us, it is a place of blessing, it is a place of favor, and it is a sign of faith. If you can't stop working because you are always worried that you're going to fail and that things won't work out if you rest, then you are not in faith. If you can never stop working, you're not in faith.

Resting is not a license to be lazy. We see the consequences of laziness all throughout the Bible. There are many Proverbs about it, and even Jesus associated laziness with wickedness (see Proverbs 12:24,27; 15:19; 20:4; 26:13-16; Matthew 25:26). However, the Bible does tell you that you need to rest. The Bible doesn't say, "Thou shalt never take a day off." The Bible talks about resting.

In the previous chapter, we covered the concept of forced rest. We looked at how the Israelites were taken out of the land into exile so that the land could have a forced rest because they had not followed God's command to rest, due to their lack of faith.

Many people's physical bodies are suffering from sickness and limitation—they are under a forced rest because they never take time to rest their bodies or minds. (Ceasing from physical activity doesn't mean your mind automatically rests. We'll talk more about this in Chapter 4.)

WORK OR TOIL?

Faith works best from a place of rest. Dr. Bill Winston once said, "The things of God work best in a garden environment." What does that mean? Let's examine how God created the original Garden of Eden:

> For in six days the Lord made the heavens and the earth, and on the seventh day He rested and was refreshed.
>
> —Exodus 31:17 (NKJV)

Exodus 31 is describing what happened in Genesis 2. You are familiar with the story of Creation, in which God created the heavens and the earth and on the seventh day, He rested. In Exodus, it says that He rested and was refreshed. We'll dig into this in a moment.

Now, I have a question. When God created the heavens and the earth, was it work or toil? When you're imagining God creating the heavens and the earth, imagine the scripture coming to pass. Was God exhausted and worn out when He finished making the heavens and earth and could just barely make it to the seventh day?

Consider those two questions: When God created the heavens and the earth, was it work or toil? And did creating the heavens and the earth wear out the almighty God? Think about those two questions as we read the account in Genesis 2:

Thus the heavens and the earth, and all the host of them, were finished. And on the seventh day God ended His work which He had done, and He rested on the seventh day from all His work which He had done. Then God blessed the seventh day and sanctified it, because in it He rested from all His work which God had created and made.

This is the history of the heavens and the earth when they were created, in the day that the Lord God made the earth and the heavens, before any plant of the field was in the earth and before any herb of the field had grown. For the Lord God had not caused it to rain on the earth, and there was no man to till the ground; but a mist went up from the earth and watered the whole face of the ground.

And the Lord God formed man of the dust of the ground, and breathed into his nostrils the breath of life; and man became a living being.

The Lord God planted a garden eastward in Eden, and there He put the man whom He had formed. And out of the ground the Lord God made every tree grow that is pleasant to the sight and good for food. The tree of life was also in the midst of the garden, and the tree of the knowledge of good and evil.

…Then the Lord God took the man and put him in the garden of Eden to tend and keep it.

—Genesis 2:1–9,15 (NKJV)

Mankind was made on the sixth day. At some point on the sixth day, Adam and Eve began their assignment. That's the day they were created, received their assignment, their authority, and the blessing of

God. They started working toward the fulfillment of their assignment on the sixth day.

However, the first full day mankind ever experienced was the seventh day. God had declared the seventh day holy because that's when He rested. So the first full day mankind ever experienced was the day of rest.

Let's take this a little further. When you read Genesis 1, it measures time by referring to the "evening and morning." That is actually how the Sabbath day is still tracked today. Sabbath begins at sundown. Knowing this, we realize that mankind was created not too long before the day ended. God's original design for mankind in the Garden was that each day begins with rest.

Adam began his assignment to work the ground, to protect the garden, to operate in dominion, and by implication expand the garden to fill the earth. Notice that in Genesis 1:26-28 he was working and copying the work schedule of the heavenly Father. Toil was not in the earth.

Toil did not come into the earth until Genesis 3, after Adam and Eve sinned and the curse came into the earth. The word used in Genesis 3 is *issabon*, "toil" or "sorrow," and it does not appear before the Fall (Strong's H6093). But in Genesis 1 and 2, Adam was commanded to work and then to rest, even though there was no toil.

Notice the pattern of God. Before toil was ever involved, Adam and Eve were still supposed to rest. Mankind was supposed to rest.

Sometimes we think we're only supposed to rest when we're worn out and exhausted. If you're worn out and exhausted, yes, there's a sign you need to rest. However, we shouldn't wait until we get to that point. We have to get into the rhythm of rest in which we're rightly taking the rest we should. God has called us to have regular times of rest.

It is vain for you to rise up early, to sit up late, to eat the bread of *sorrows*; for so He gives His beloved sleep.

—Psalm 127:2 (NKJV)

Here the word *sorrows* is the word *esab*, which means "painful toil" (Strong's H6089). It comes from the same root word as *issabon*, which is *asab* (Strong's H6087). The psalm is describing a worthless way to live—getting up super early and staying up late to toil. It's not saying you shouldn't get up early or stay up late. But what is the purpose of living that way? If it is to toil so that you can enjoy the fruit of toil, it is vain—meaning that it will all come to nothing. The word used here, *sav*, means emptiness, desolation, nothingness (Strong's H7723). If you live by toiling and you don't rest, it will become nothing.

> The blessing of the Lord makes one rich, and He adds no sorrow [eseb] with it.
> —Proverbs 10:22 (NKJV)

Some people believe that the only way they can get rich is through sorrow and painful toil. The blessing of the Lord is God's empowerment to prosper. When you live God's way, He blesses the work of your hands and puts extra blessing on your life so that you can rest. This way, you have more than enough without painful toil.

This isn't everyone's case, but could it be possible that you're not experiencing the blessing of the Lord because you refuse to rest? Refusing to rest is violating your body. Refusing to rest shows that you don't have faith in your covenant. Remember, the ability to rest is a sign of your covenant.

If you have the mentality that you have to do everything and that nobody is going to help you, and if, "I have to do everything by myself, by myself, no one else," has become your constant mantra, then you have programmed yourself to keep working in your own strength until you have a physical or mental breakdown. You are making sure that something will happen in your body that will force you to slow down.

This rest thing is serious. This rest thing is holy. This rest thing is God's idea. Your body was made to rest. Are you allowing yourself to rest? This does not just mean an annual vacation for a change of scenery—we're talking about taking regular times to rest.

THE REST THAT GOD GIVES

"God gives His beloved sleep." When you can work hard and, at the end of the day, say, "You know what? I'm going to go sleep well"—that is a gift from God. Making a decision to rest is an act of faith, believing, "I've done my part, and God blesses the work of my hands, so now I'm going to rest."

Rest is not only for your body. You have to rest your mind, too. How? By taking control of your thoughts as Paul teaches in 2 Corinthians 10:3–5. You have to take control of all anxious thoughts. As you read through this book, I'll share in Chapter 4 how you can conquer anxious and intrusive thoughts that rob you of God's rest.

Where do you experience rest the best? I challenge you to use your faith on this. You may say, "Well, I rest the most by going to the beach." Then how often do you need to go to the beach? Is every other year, or even one week out of each year, enough to get you filled up on beach rest?

You may say, "I rest by going to the mountains." Then how often do you need to go to the mountains?

Do you need to consider moving and getting yourself closer to some mountains?

Maybe there is some other place or activity that helps you rest. The question remains the same in every case: how often do you need to do that?

You have to examine your life. Pay attention to your life. Pay attention to your mental health, your physical health, and everything going on in your life. Start jotting these things down.

Some people don't get what they want in life because they don't ask for it in faith. On the other hand, a lot of people don't ask for things because they don't know they need them.

They think, "Well, I can't ask for a vacation. It's not really the will of God for me to take a break." Yes, it is the will of God for you to take a break. Do you need it? Yes, you do. You need to be willing to reorganize your life to experience the rhythm of rest.

You may have a million seemingly valid reasons why you can't rest, why you can't take a break. Those reasons will never change. If you keeping saying,

"One day when, one day when, one day when…" that one day will never come. Later, you will have problems in your body and you'll be forced to stop. As a result, you won't be able to enjoy the rest because of the state of your physical body or the state of your soul and your mental health.

Before burnout forces you to stop, figure out how to reorganize your life. You have to ask yourself the following question and honestly answer it: how are you going to rest?

You might say, "Well, I can't have a day when I just completely do nothing."

I'm not saying that you need to have a day when you completely do nothing. I'm saying that you need to have a day when you rest. What does a day of rest look like to you? You need to write that down. Maybe you need to take a walk or plan a specific activity that helps you rest. Figure out what works for you, because everyone rests differently.

If I were to describe my day of rest, you might reply, "I could not do that. That does not sound enjoyable to me."

If you described your day of rest to someone else, they might reply, "Why would anybody ever want to do that?"

You have to find out what a day of rest looks like for you. If you're married or you have kids, what does it look like for your family unit? Make sure you take that rest. If you do not take time to rest and refresh, you have crossed over into toil and your faith is not working the way it was intended to. You've crossed over into a lifestyle that will produce vanity and nothing, and you won't enjoy the results of it.

Sadly, so many people toil, toil, toil, and when they finally get to where they're going they can't enjoy it. In Ecclesiastes, the Scriptures tell us that it is the gift of God for you to enjoy the fruit of your labor and the work of your hands (Ecclesiastes 5:18-20).

Why would you toil so hard that you don't enjoy what you're doing? God wants you to enjoy the work of your hands, but you're only going to enjoy it if you actually take regular time to rest. You can't just rest once a year.

By paying attention to my own life over the last several years, one of the things I found out is that I can't just wait for a certain time of year to rest. My mentality can't be, "I'm going to catch up on all my rest that week." That's not the healthy way to live. It's better than not resting at all; however, it is not God's best for us. You have to make time to get into the regular rhythm of rest.

There will always be reasons why you can't rest, but you're going to have to make a decision to rest anyway. Similarly, there are always reasons why you can't eat healthy, but you have to make sure that you eat healthy anyway. There will always be reasons why you can't walk in love, but you have to walk in love anyway. There will always be reasons why you can't budget or save money, but you still have to do it anyway. There will always be reasons not to do what you're supposed to do, but you have to do it anyway.

If you do not regularly take time to rest and refresh, you are living a lifestyle of toil. In the next chapter, we'll talk more about how toil is caused by lack of faith and the connection between faith and resting.

REFLECTION QUESTIONS

Consider these questions and write down your answers in your journal.

1. What was the first full day that Adam and Eve experienced?
2. In understanding that rest was God's original plan for mankind, how does that impact your thinking regarding your rest habits?
3. How are you going to rest?
4. What times or days will you regularly take time to rest?
5. Where and when do you experience rest the best?
6. What does a perfect day of rest look like for you?
7. What in this chapter impacted you the most?

A PRAYER FOR YOU TO PRAY

Father, reveal to me the ways that I should rest. Show me the best way for me to rest. You know me even better than I do. Help me to understand how to experience the rest You have for me. I receive Your help and wisdom. Thank You! In Jesus' Name, amen.

CHAPTER 3

FAITH AND REST

～

*But that no one is justified by the law in the sight of
God is evident, for "the just shall live by faith."*
—Galatians 3:11 (NKJV)

Is your lack of rest a sign of a lack of faith? First, let's
define faith. In my Faith Bible Institute and in my
Faith+ courses, I share that faith is defined as firm
belief, confidence, assurance, firm persuasion, the con-
viction of the truth of anything, belief with the pre-
dominate idea of trust. Faith is mentioned 245 times
in the New Testament, which should give a great
insight into how we as Christians are called to live.

Habakkuk 2:4, Galatians 3:11, Romans 1:17, and
Hebrews 10:38 all declare that the just live by faith.

Faith is more than a moment or a movement. It is a lifestyle. A *lifestyle* is simply the way a person lives. It is determined by what a person does consistently.

Romans 10:17 tells us that faith comes to our heart as we continually hear God's Word. Is your lack of rest a sign of a lack of faith? You might say, "I don't lack faith! I have faith. I am a faith person. I read God's Word. I can quote Scriptures about rest!" Look at what Hebrews 3:19 says:

> So we see that because of their unbelief they were not able to enter his rest.
>
> —Hebrews 3:19 (NLT)

This verse is referring to the first generation of Israelites who came out of Egypt with Moses. It should have taken them only about two years to get to the Promised Land, because God took them on a slower route. When they arrived at the edge of the Promised Land, they refused to enter. How does Hebrews 3:19 sum up that incident? They did not enter the Promised Land because they refused to believe God.

The Promised Land was called God's rest. It was called their inheritance. The first generation of Israelites missed out on God's rest because of their unbelief. Yes, there were battles in the Promised Land. Yes, there was work to be done in the Promised Land, but it was far better than Egypt and the wilderness. They missed out on God's rest because they refused to believe. Are you missing out on God's rest and God's best because you refuse to believe?

Therefore, since a promise remains of entering His rest, let us fear lest any of you seem to have come short of it. For indeed the gospel was preached to us as well as to them; but the word which they heard did not profit them, not being mixed with faith in those who heard it. For we who have believed do enter that rest, as He has said: "So I swore in My wrath, 'They shall not enter My rest,'" although the works were finished from the foundation of the world. For He has spoken in a certain place of the seventh day in this way: "And God rested on the seventh day from all His works"; and again in this place: "They shall not enter My rest."

Since therefore it remains that some must enter it, and those to whom it was first preached did not enter because of disobedience, again He designates a certain day, saying in David, "Today," after such a long time, as it has been said:

"Today, if you will hear His voice, do not harden your hearts."

For if Joshua had given them rest, then He would not afterward have spoken of another day. There remains therefore a rest for the people of God. For he who has entered His rest has himself also ceased from his works as God did from His. Let us therefore be diligent to enter that rest, lest anyone fall according to the same example of disobedience.

—Hebrews 4:1-11 (NKJV)

There are many different types of rest God has made available for believers. There is more than the eternal blessed rest of Heaven. There's rest for you on this earth, but you can miss out on all of God's rest if you refuse to believe.

BELIEVING FOR A GOOD NIGHT'S SLEEP

You may feel kind of defensive reading through this book. You might say, "Well, pastor, I'm not taking a forced rest. My body is good. My body is strong." But how is your mind? How are your emotions? If your soul becomes weary and burdened with strain and anxiety, your body may be okay for a while, but you will still end up in a forced rest.

> It is useless for you to work so hard from early morning until late at night, anxiously working for food to eat; for God gives rest to his loved ones.
>
> —Psalm 127:2 (NLT)

I understand that sometimes you might have to pull an all-nighter, but that can't be every night. The

Bible says it is worthless, useless, and vain to live that way. Instead, God gives those He loves sleep. Proverbs 3:24 (NKJV) describes that sleep as sweet sleep:

> When you lie down, you will not be afraid; yes, you will lie down and your sleep will be sweet.

God wants you to enjoy sweet sleep. Your sleep is not supposed to be troubled. You are redeemed from any trouble sleeping. Under the old covenant, the Bible says your sleep is supposed to be sweet. How much better should your sleep be under the new covenant?

I still remember when I was in college. My brother and I attended the same school at the same time. I was on one floor, he was on another. Anytime one of his friends would have trouble sleeping, he would tell them, "Go upstairs and talk to my brother."

They would come up to talk to me, and I would take them to Psalm 127:2 and Proverbs 3:24. I taught them what the Bible said about their sleep—God wants you to rest. God wants you to sleep. I showed them how to use their God-given authority to go to sleep. Then I would instruct them to pray a prayer I would give them and they would have the best sleep of their life that night. They would do it, and it would work every single time. They would come back to my brother and say things like, "Dude, I slept for hours."

Before we progress further into this chapter, I want to teach you the prayer I taught these gentlemen many years ago.

PRAYER FOR THOSE WHO HAVE TROUBLE SLEEPING

Father, I believe You love me. In Psalm 127:2, You said that You give those You love sleep. Because of Your wisdom, You said in Proverbs 3:24 that when I lie down, I will not be afraid and when I lie down my sweet will be sleep. Father, according to these Scriptures I ask for the sweet sleep of the beloved. I receive the sweet sleep and I thank You for it. I bind and rebuke bad dreams and bad thoughts, wicked dreams and wicked thoughts, and any form of nightmares or terror from the enemy. My sleep is sweet because my

God loves me. I sleep through the night and I wake up refreshed. In Jesus' Name, amen.

PLANNING WITH PURPOSE

Faith is displayed in the words of your mouth *and* the actions of your life. Faith is more than just words. Faith is shown by your works when you put your words into action. We should believe God's promises for a long and satisfying life. They are repeated in Scripture time and time again. But your belief should go beyond what you say—it should impact your mentality, which should affect how you view and plan your life.

A lack of a planning, discipline, vision, and self-control will cause you to toil when you should be resting and enjoying the fruit of your labor. You have to make a plan to rest. A lot of people live aimlessly and do random things because they don't have a plan. You need to plan your day.

Now, I'm not saying you have to be the person who plans every single minute. If you're that type of person who can plan every single minute and execute it, then knock yourself out and enjoy it. However, for the rest of us, you should at least come up with a list of things you need to do and a comprehensive plan to get your list done. And part of that list needs to be your plan for rest and taking a break.

As you make a list, you know that you have a certain set number of work hours in which you need to get certain things done. In between those work hours, can you take a walk? Is taking a walk for five to ten minutes a good mental health break for you? Planning and taking moments of rest throughout the day and making sure you rest at night is part of the rhythm of rest.

Don't say, "Oh, no, I can't do that." Stop saying what you can't do. Figure out what you can do. Many times we don't enjoy what God has for us because we have all the reasons in the world why we can't. Let's find a reason why we can.

My good friend Pastor David Winston says that we cannot have long-life beliefs with short-life habits. Think about that. What does he mean by long-life beliefs and short-life habits?

A lot of believers I know have goals to live long and live strong. They aim to live 120 years and correctly quote Psalm 91:16, saying, "God will satisfy me with long life and show me His salvation." They have the correct daily affirmations and overall beliefs. However, if they refuse to rest, they have long-life beliefs with short-life habits.

We cannot have long-life beliefs with short-life habits. If you're eating, living, and working in a way that contributes to only a 60-year lifespan, then you will not see the long life God has for you, even though the promise of God is true.

Toiling is a short-life habit, and it produces short-life diets. Some people make poor health decisions, such as eating a short-life diet, because they don't know how to rest. You know what I mean by a short-life diet. It's fast food. It's food chosen for convenience and comfort rather than balanced nutrition that serves your body's needs. If unhealthy grab-and-go food is a lifestyle with you, then you are not living in rest and you're not choosing a long-life diet.

When it comes to planning times of rest, here's how that mentality sounds: "Because I plan to live a long time, I'm going to take a day off. Because I plan to live a long time, I'm going to rest. Because I plan to live a long time, I'm going to take care of my mental health. Because I plan to live a long time, I'm going on vacation. Because I plan to live a long time, I'm going to sleep tonight."

You cannot have short-life habits and expect them to support your long-life beliefs. It won't work. You're going to have to put some action to your faith. Yes, it's good to go over the Scriptures and remind yourself that He'll satisfy you with long life and show you His salvation. Don't stop doing that. But in addition to that, develop the habits that lead to a long life.

It's faith and works. As the Book of James teaches, faith without works is dead (James 2:17). Don't hold long-life beliefs while choosing short-life habits. Have long-life habits with long-life beliefs. And one of the long-life habits you have to embrace is the rhythm of rest.

You have to be led by the Spirit of God if you are going to stay in the rhythm of rest for your life. You have to be sensitive to the leading of the Spirit of God. When He tells you to stop working, you stop. When He tells you go to bed, you go to bed. When He tells you to put down your phone, you put down your phone. When He tells you to go do additional work, you go work. When He tells you focus on a certain thing, you focus on that. When He tells you to pick up the pace, you pick up the pace. When He tells you to slow down the pace, you slow down the pace. The Holy Spirit will help you develop the plan you need to rest. As the plan develops, you will be able to break the plan into actionable steps and have a vision for your rest.

Once you have a plan, you commit to that plan. You treat rest as holy and guard your times of rest. I understand that emergencies pop up, but that shouldn't be your everyday life. Some emergencies show up because of poor planning. When you execute your plan with self-control and discipline, you eliminate certain emergencies.

Some people are constantly putting out proverbial fires and are not able to stop and rest. They didn't make the proper plans ahead of time. Then everything becomes urgent and an emergency. Instead of living life, they are running on adrenaline, cortisol, stress, and their body is breaking down. Sadly, they continue to think they are enjoying life because they are used to the chemical high in their bodies caused by all the hormones that stress produces.

Hebrews 4:11 (MEV) tells us, "Let us labor therefore to enter that rest, lest anyone fall by the same pattern of unbelief." Entering into the rhythm of rest is work. It's not automatic. You need to have a vision for your life. It's going to take discipline. It's going to take self-control, and yes, it's going to take faith.

FIGHT FOR YOUR REST

Now, from time to time, the enemy will try to stir up something to keep you from resting. When that happens, use the authority given to you in the name of Jesus to bind the activity of the enemy so that you can enjoy the benefits of rest God has made available to you. In the next chapter, I will share with you how you can effectively use your God-given authority to stop the enemy's interference in your life and protect your rest.

Rest is essential for all of us, no matter our profession. If you are a human, God says you have to rest. There's no profession or spiritual office where you are exempt from resting. Some people think that ministers, apostles, prophets, evangelists, pastors, and teachers don't need to rest. Not so—they need to rest, too. Government leaders need to rest. Educators need to rest. We all need to rest. No matter your profession, no matter your place of leadership, no matter your place of influence, you need to rest. Refusing to rest will shorten your lifespan and, therefore, the span of your authority, your influence, and your impact. If you want longevity in your calling, you need to rest.

We all have to take time to rest. The long-life habit of rest includes habitual restoration and renewal. We all have to figure out what is rest for us. As you grow, as you age, what is rest for you may change. When you notice the change, make the change needed so you can stay in the rhythm of rest for your life.

There are many people who die early because they don't rest. It doesn't mean they weren't anointed. It doesn't mean they weren't successful. It doesn't mean they didn't have faith. It was that they refused to rest their bodies. You can't only make the decision to rest when you're older. You have to make this decision before your body needs it, before you're in a forced rest.

REFLECTION QUESTIONS

Take some time to consider these questions and answer them in your journal.

1. What is faith?
2. How is faith displayed?
3. In your life, have you refused to rest because there was a lack of faith on your part?
4. What short-life habits do you need to change?
5. What are some decisions that you need to make today?

6. How do you plan to implement what you learned in this chapter?
7. What stood out to you the most in this chapter?
8. What is your plan to rest? Write down detailed steps on how to implement your plan.

A PRAYER FOR YOU TO PRAY

Father, I believe You! Reveal to me where I have short-life habits and help me to make the necessary changes. I believe You have rest for me. I want to experience it. I pray that You help me develop and implement the plan so that I can live in Your rhythm of rest for my life. In Jesus' Name, amen.

CHAPTER 4

THE LORD OF THE SABBATH

A *rhythm* is a strong, regular, repeated pattern of movement or sound. It's something you do regularly. Although we're not required to keep a certain day of rest under our new covenant, we have to get into the rhythm of rest.

Well, how are you supposed to do it? What day? What time? The Sabbath was not created as a list of rules for you to follow. Mankind was not made for the Sabbath, but Sabbath was made for mankind. When Jesus said this, He shocked the religious leaders of His day. He also identified Himself as the Lord of the Sabbath.

How do you enter the rest for your life? You come to Jesus. What did He say in Matthew 11?

Are you tired? Worn out? Burned out on religion? Come to me. Get away with me and
you'll recover your life. I'll show you how to
take a real rest. Walk with me and work with
me—watch how I do it. Learn the unforced
rhythms of grace. I won't lay anything heavy or
ill-fitting on you. Keep company with me and
you'll learn to live freely and lightly.

—Matthew 11:28-30 (MSG)

In learning that there are "unforced rhythms of
grace," you learn that there is a rhythm to your rest.
Now, you may not be required to keep the Sabbath
day or a Sabbath year, but you have to learn to rest.
When the Israelites were too busy every Sabbath to
rest, that was their rhythm.

There is a rhythm of rest for your life, too. There
are times when everything should be fast-paced. You
might say, "Well, I don't like fast-paced." But there
are times when you have to move fast. There are also
times when you have to move slow. Which is which?
When you follow the Holy Spirit, He'll tell you to

speed up. He'll tell you to slow down. He'll tell you to do nothing. He'll tell you to get up and do something. He'll tell you to go on vacation.

The rhythm to your rest is the rhythm of grace. It is the rhythm of following the Spirit of God and actually acknowledging Him in all your ways. There may be many valid reasons why you have never learned to rest, but you have to learn now before your body is put on a forced rest.

Do not allow the enemy or your culture to tell you that you cannot rest. Do not buy the lie that tells you the only way you can rest is through smoking weed or some other damaging habit. Sedatives do not equal a vacation, and they will trap you.

Don't say that you can't rest because you work in a toxic workplace or have a bad boss. Although those two things can be challenges and contribute to making rest difficult, for most people it isn't their boss or their job. It's them and their mentality. If every job is too hard and every environment is toxic, then the problem isn't the boss or the job. It's that person.

If you are currently working in a challenging, even toxic, workplace, are you taking your toxic patterns and toiling mentality into that workplace? Even if you are not in that type of workplace, do you blame your boss because you had time off and you still couldn't rest? Do you keep blaming your spouse or your kids? If it is always someone else's fault that you cannot rest, there is a common denominator. It's you. As you read through this book, make a decision in your heart that you will experience the rest God has for you no matter what the challenges are in your life.

SCHEDULING SABBATHS

As we look at the concept of the Sabbath under the old covenant, we learn that it is a wise practice to take time every week to not work. That doesn't mean you do nothing, because in this life, you still have to do something. You're still going to have to eat, right? You still might have to do something with the kids. But what you need to do is to set a pace for that day that's different than your workdays. Whatever your job schedule is, you have to pick a day and say, "This is my Sabbath. This is my rest." It doesn't matter whether it's Friday or Saturday or Tuesday.

Now, because of the schedules and demands of life, that day could change from week to week. However, you still need to get into the rhythm of the spirit of grace for your life and pick a day and say, "Today, I'm not doing all the other stuff I normally do."

That decision, mentality, and rhythm will preserve and lengthen your life. If you are a person whose mind is always racing, you have to learn to tell your mind to calm down.

You might say, "Well, I get my best ideas at night." Let's examine—why are you so creative at that time? You might be a night owl and are creative at night. That's fine. You might be a morning person and you are creative in the morning. Examine and pay attention to yourself. Why are you creative at this time? Why are you getting ideas? Is it a certain time of the day, or is it because you finally stopped moving and got into a still position—you finally put distractions away? Why are you really creative and productive at that time?

If it's because you're finally still and you put aside the distractions, then make time for that throughout the day so that you can get your ideas out, capitalize on that creativity, and still enjoy rest at night. You have to approach your life with a different mentality and be willing to restructure. Plan to go to bed just a little bit earlier. Bring your notebook with you to bed so you can jot down those ideas. By the time the creativity stops, you go to sleep.

If you don't consider yourself creative, remember your heavenly Father is creative and you're made in His image. You have to pay attention to yourself to know when you are most creative. Guard that time so you can keep being creative and then structure your life around it.

This is not a foreign concept. You structure your life to go to work and get your job done. You have to take the same mindset when it comes to creativity. Creativity is an important part of you enjoying the rhythm of rest for your life. If you're creative, you'll be more productive.

You are not a hamster in a hamster wheel. You're not supposed to keep running until you don't have any energy or power left. The hamster is not producing anything. It's time for you to get off the hamster wheel of life and become creatively productive.

When we think about the ministry of Jesus and study it, we see that He traveled to many places far apart. At times, He and his team were moving at a fast place as they were covering a lot of distance. However, as we read the Gospels, we see that the Son of God would take breaks and rest. He even took all of His apostles on a vacation to step away from the demand and busyness of ministry. Jesus was only in ministry for three years and He took frequent breaks. If He did it, you might need to follow that example.

Remember, we have a new covenant. Our Sabbath rest is not a hard, set law to rest on a certain day. In this new covenant, you have to get into the rhythm of grace for your life. You have to pay attention to your life. You have to learn when you are the most creative. You have to discern when you are the most productive.

Times of creativity and productivity differ from person to person. It can be different for every single one of us. In order for you to create, so that you can produce, so that you can make a difference, you have to discover yourself.

WHAT'S YOUR REST?

How do you rest? All of us rest differently. For some, if you sat down and literally did nothing, you'd be that hyper person on the couch just bouncing your legs all day. As soon as the rest day was over, you would be thrilled because you didn't actually rest at all. You ceased from activity, but you did not rest. Yes, you need to sleep, but you also need to find out how you rest.

My wife and I were talking about this recently. When we go on vacation, we have different versions of rest and what is refreshing. I'm a very energetic person. Some people might say that I'm hyper, and they wonder why I even drink coffee and who was responsible for introducing me to coffee.

Are you like that? If you are a person like me, your view of rest may be different. For me to rest,

I need an adventure. I like going to new places. I will work out even if I'm resting on vacation. I will hit the gym, get ready, and look forward to the next activity. What am I doing? I'm resting in my mind. That's what I need.

You may be a person who needs to take a vacation and just sit by the pool all day. That's the way you rest. It's important for you to discover what type of rest you need and get into that rhythm of rest.

Here's another question connected to the rhythm of rest that you need to answer: how often do you need to change the scenery? When you understand how God made you, you can set your faith and have that as your reality. You're not trying to copy somebody else's vacation. You're not envious of somebody else's beach house or travel schedule. You will realize that occasionally changing the scene of your life is not just a desire, but it is a need because of how God made you.

What does Philippians 4:19 (NKJV) tell us? "God shall supply all your need according to His riches in glory." If you don't know you have a need, you won't set your faith to receive it. Here are a number of additional questions I want you to consider:

- How often do you need to go somewhere?
- How often do you need to change the scenery?
- How often do you need to go to the mountains?
- How often do you need to go to the beach?
- How often do you need to go to the city?
- How often do you need to have an adventure?

Pay attention to yourself and start writing these things down so that you can release your faith to walk into this reality. God has more for you, but if you just keep doing what you're doing, you won't be able to go the distance. The plan of God for your life spans several decades. You're going to have to learn how to rest along the way if you want to not just complete the call on your life, but also enjoy it.

THE WITNESS OF REST

What is our witness to the world? What do they see when they consider our lives? Do you really think it's a good idea, a good witnessing tool, or a good testimony to always live a life that says, "Oh, I'm just working for Jesus. Oh, I'm so tired. I'll rest when I'm dead and get into Heaven. The sinners look like they're enjoying their life."

That's not a good witnessing tool. That's not a billboard that screams "Choose Jesus." Are you out of rhythm? Even if you cannot clap on beat, you should not live off beat. It's time for you to get into the rhythm of rest for your life.

You'll grow in understanding of your rhythm as you pay attention to your life, acknowledge the Lord, and allow Him to direct your path (Proverbs 3:6). As you follow His directions, God will give you favor.

When I take breaks, there's so, so much favor on me. You might say, "That's because they know you're a pastor." But when I travel, most people don't know who I am or what I do. They just know they want to bless me. I am constantly blessed with upgrades, bigger rooms, and rooms with a view.

I remember checking in to a hotel one time. They asked if they could put us on one of the top floors so we could overlook Broadway and see all of New York City. I gratefully accepted. I did not ask for it. It was the favor of God. Did we pay a lot? No. It was the favor of God following God's principle of rest.

I make the decision to take a rest because God says I should. I believe, know, and expect that when I rest, I'm going to be blessed. Years ago, when we had only been pastoring for a year or two, we experienced an extended, intense period of work. A lot had been going on at the church and we needed to take a break. We hadn't planned a break, but we needed to take one. I had not yet fully learned the principles I'm sharing with you in this book. However, I knew we needed to rest, so I started looking for special deals online.

We found this cruise line and they had a special deal on the last room on the boat. And I mean the *last* room on the boat. We booked the room. We drove to the port, boarded the boat, and we were on the bottom level. There was no sunlight, but we didn't care because we were so exhausted. In the bottom of the ship, we were tossing back and forth, but we didn't notice. It rocked us to sleep. That's how exhausted we were.

After catching up with some sleep, I was ready to do things and go out for an adventure, but it was a day at sea. I woke up early in the morning and thought, "Well, I'm resting. What do I like to do? I like good views and I like coffee. While I'm doing that, I want to read through all of Paul's epistles."

I found the perfect spot. I sat there and looked out the expansive windows. Every time I went out there, I saw whales jumping out in the ocean. It was the favor of God.

While I sat there, I would finish a cup of coffee and think, "Let me go get another." The staff would stop me and say, "No, no, no, sir. You're doing important work. We got you." What was I doing? I was resting, reading the Scriptures, and the blessing and the favor just kept working.

You might say, "Well, you took all this time to pray and rest. God must have been talking to you about the church."

No, He wasn't. He would talk to me about me. He didn't talk to me about what to preach until the last day of that cruise because He knew I needed to rest. Why would the Holy Ghost violate the principle of rest? He didn't talk to me about work-related things until it was time for work again.

MY PRAYER FOR THOSE WHO ARE BELIEVING TO GO ON A VACATION

Father, I pray, I release my faith now for people who are believing to take a vacation, but they need certain things to line up. I pray that those things line up. I pray that all the money comes in. I pray that they will take a vacation that they enjoy. I pray that as they go on vacation their experiences are upgraded, that favor is granted toward them, and that they're able to take a real rest. I plead the blood of Jesus over every mode of transportation and resort and place where they go to and stay. Angels, go forth and secure these things and bring them to these people quickly. In Jesus' Name, amen.

If you are in agreement with my prayer, say "Amen."

FRUITFUL REST

You need to get into the rhythm of rest. You need to get into the rhythm of the Spirit of grace. Under the law, God gave them the Sabbath year and told them not to work their land for that whole year, and He would extraordinarily bless them so that their harvest would cover three years. If God could do that under an old covenant, an inferior covenant, a covenant that was based on your performance, what can He do under a new covenant, a time of grace full of faith and the Holy Ghost? What can He produce in your life? If you get into the rhythm of grace, the rhythm of rest, how much more productive will you be? How much more creative will you be? How much more prosperous will you be?

When we are living in the rhythm of rest, we are following the example that the Lord of the Sabbath outlines in Matthew 11:28–30. You have to get into this rhythm, which is set by the Holy Spirit.

Then Jesus said, "Come to me, all of you who are weary and carry heavy burdens, and I will give you rest. Take my yoke upon you. Let me teach you, because I am humble and gentle at heart, and you will find rest for your souls. For my yoke is easy to bear, and the burden I give you is light."

—Matthew 11:28-30 (NLT)

Come to Me, all you who labor and are heavy-laden and overburdened, and I will cause you to rest. [I will ease and relieve and refresh your souls.] Take My yoke upon you and learn of Me, for I am gentle (meek) and humble (lowly) in heart, and you will find rest (relief and ease and refreshment and recreation and blessed quiet) for your souls. For My yoke is wholesome (useful, good—not harsh, hard, sharp, or pressing, but comfortable, gracious, and pleasant), and My burden is light and easy to be borne.

—Matthew 11:28-30 (AMPC)

In this passage, Jesus said that you should take His yoke upon you. A yoke was placed on two cattle and caused them to work closely side by side. With that in mind, Jesus said, "Learn of Me. Let me teach you. Watch how I do it." Why would He tell you to watch? Because He's close. The rhythm of rest is a life of close partnership between you and the Lord.

Jesus continued and described Himself as meek. In describing Himself as meek, He was saying, "I have My emotions in check." If you want to enjoy the rest God has for you, you have to control your emotions. If you are always going off on everybody, yelling at everyone, and are always losing your cool, you will not enjoy the rest God has for you. If you don't have your emotions in check, you will lose your rest. You have to grow to a point where you do not allow things to easily set you off. If any social media post, news report, or anything can easily set you off, you are in a dangerous place and you have lost your rest.

Think about it this way. You had a whole day off. You had a great plan for that day off. But someone posted something off-putting on your social media feed. As a result, you are fuming. You are upset, mad, depressed, and filling your mind with what you saw. Something trivial just stole something important from you.

Is that a pattern in your life? If every time you take a day off, something bad happens and you can't rest, that's the enemy. You must use your God-given authority in the name of Jesus and stop that.

I learned how to do this in my early teen years. As a young teenage boy, I really liked my family's Thanksgiving food. I still do! But for a couple of years in a row, every time Thanksgiving was about to start, I would get sick, I would lose my appetite, and then I would lose my voice.

This began to happen after I received my call to ministry. My mom pointed something out to me that I never forgot. She said, "Every time you get sick, you lose your voice. That's an attack of the enemy because he doesn't want you to talk. You have to use your authority and stop that."

What did I do? I used my authority and said, "I'm not losing my voice and I'm going to enjoy that

Thanksgiving meal." Guess what happened? I never had that issue again.

You have to begin to look at your life this way and look for patterns of disruption. Some people just accept disruptions and say, "Oh, that's just life." Stop letting life happen to you. Go happen to life. As a believer in the Lord Jesus Christ, you have authority. You have to use your authority and stop the attacks of the enemy arrayed against you.

Now, I'm not telling you just to start yelling out, "In the Name, in the Name!" That has some type of impact, but I want to share with you how to get the maximum impact from your authority.

Back up a little bit from the situation and say, "All right, Holy Ghost, I see this pattern. What do I need to do to stop it? What do I need to say to this mountain?" Do you remember what Jesus did in Mark 11? In Mark 11:14 (KJV), He spoke to the fig tree and it dried up from the root: "No man eat fruit of thee hereafter for ever."

In Mark 11:23 (KJV), He said, "For verily I say unto you, That whosoever shall say unto this mountain, *Be thou removed, and be thou cast into the sea*; and shall not doubt in his heart, but shall believe that those things which he saith shall come to pass; he shall have whatsoever he saith." In Greek, He only needed six words to issue that command.

Jesus didn't come up with those words. As you study the passage, you realize that Jesus walked by the fig tree once, walked away, and the next day came back and spoke to it. Where did those words come from? The Father. Jesus said in the Gospel of John, "I only say what I hear My Father say. I only do what I see Him do" (see John 5:19; 12:49).

To fully follow the example of the Lord of the Sabbath in Mark 11:23, you have to get your words from the Father just like Jesus did. That's why I said you have to back up, pray, and ask for your instructions. When you see a disruptive pattern of mountains popping up in your life, follow this example from the Lord of the Sabbath. As you do, the Holy Spirit will lead you in what to say and what to do.

A PRAYER TO DAILY PRAY TO EXERCISE YOUR GOD-GIVEN AUTHORITY IN THE NAME OF JESUS

Father, I thank You for giving me authority in the Name of Jesus. According to Ephesians 1 and 2, I take my place in Christ seated at Your right hand in the heavenly places. In the name of Jesus, I bind the plans of the enemy to disrupt my life, steal my rest, and interfere in what You have called my family and me to. I plead the blood of Jesus over every area of my life— spiritually, emotionally, mentally, physically, socially, and financially. Father, I am open to anything else that I should speak to the situations and circumstances in my life. Grant me the words to say. Thank You for giving me authority and victory over the enemy. In Jesus' Name, amen.

AN ACCURATE VISION

Jesus also described Himself as humble. What does it mean to be humble? What is true humility? It means to be submitted to the plan of God and to think accurately about yourself. Being humble doesn't mean you think horribly about yourself. It means you think accurately about yourself. If you step outside of meekness and humility, you will step out of the rhythm of rest for your life.

If you keep living a certain pattern again and again, you need to put something else before your eyes. You need to change the image in your heart and develop a vision for your life, your rest, and what God has promised you. Get God's vision in your heart and in your mind. A vision is a clear, defined image that you are heading toward.

How do you replace wrong images of yourself and your life and develop a vision for rest? It's very simple. You don't have to be artistic. It can be a simple vision board. Post a picture of yourself smiling on the board. Surround the picture of yourself with pictures that represent rest and enjoyment—the rhythm of rest principles that you learn in this book. Look at the board every day and say, "That's me." As you do that, you are replacing the wrong image in your heart and mind.

If you don't consciously replace wrong thinking and beliefs, you will subconsciously keep producing from the wrong image in your heart and experiencing results in your life that you do not want. What does Proverbs tell us? As a man thinks in his heart, so is he (see Proverbs 23:7).

DON'T PANIC!

If your emotions are not under control, you're not operating in the fruit of meekness. Out-of-control emotions, that roller coaster of emotions, will rob you of your rest. Going up and down, being high, low, high, low, back and forth will cause you to lose out on the rest God has for you. What happens when your emotions are out of whack? What do you do? You begin to panic, and when you panic you make poor decisions. When you make poor decisions, they follow you down the road. As a result, when you should be resting, you end up toiling because you panicked.

> And you will hear of wars and threats of wars,
> but don't panic. Yes, these things must take
> place, but the end won't follow immediately.
> —Matthew 24:6 (NLT)

When you look at what Jesus said in the Gospels concerning the end times, His key command is, "Don't panic." One of the things I share with different civic, political, and economic leaders is that despite the times we're living in, cool heads will prevail.

To get through a turbulent season, you're going to need a cool head. You can't panic. You can't lose your head. You must keep your head and keep your cool. You have the helmet of salvation for a reason (Ephesians 6:17). It's time to put that on by applying the instructions of Philippians 4:6-7:

> Be anxious for nothing, but in everything by prayer and supplication, with thanksgiving, let your requests be made known to God; and the peace of God, which surpasses all understanding, will guard your hearts and minds through Christ Jesus.
>
> —Philippians 4:6-7 (NKJV)

Out-of-control emotions will rob you of your rest. When you feel anxious, don't turn to thoughts of worry. Instead, pray about it. When the Scripture talks about prayer and supplication, it means that you are making a request to God. It's a request that you make in faith, which is why it says to make this request with thanksgiving. You thank Him because you know He heard you and He's going to give you what you requested (1 John 5:14-15). Philippians 4:6-7 has to be become our habit. This habit regarding our emotions is an important part of the rhythm of rest.

When you feel worried, stressed, or anxious, turn to God. How often should you do that? Every time. Now, that doesn't mean you have to drop to your knees in the middle of the store or rush off to your prayer closet. Internally, on the inside, you keep this conversation with God going. Say, "God, I feel stressed right now. God, I feel worried right now."

Now, you may be stressed without knowing it. You may not have outright stressful thoughts, but you may notice that your body is experiencing stress. In Chapter 8, I'll share with you how to pay attention to the signals your body gives you. There are some signals that you shouldn't ignore.

What happens when you try to ignore everything and keep pushing, pushing, and pushing? When you ignore a signal and attempt to push through it and not address it, you are setting yourself up for disaster. As we'll cover later, there are some things that can be ignored, but there are some things that need to be addressed. If you're feeling stress in your body and always choose to ignore it and say, "I'm just going to watch TV and eat some ice cream, and everything will be better."

Whoa, whoa, whoa. The TV and ice cream did not change the problem. It may have given you some mental relief for a moment, but you will still need to address the problem.

Why are you feeling stressed? Now, if you know why you're feeling stressed and you know how to handle it, then that's what you do. However, sometimes you can feel stressed and not know the reason. If you are feeling stressed and don't know why, take a moment and say, "God, I feel stressed right now. I'm not sure what's going on. Father, I don't know why I feel stressed and anxious. I don't know what's going on, but I cast this anxiety on You. I cast this worry on You. I cast this care on You. I know You care for me. Help me do what I need to do. Help me focus where I need to focus. I cast this on You. I believe You love me. You're restoring my soul."

If you pray that way and live open to the Holy Spirit, He'll teach you why you feel stressed. He'll either speak to you or send the right person across your path to give you that wisdom you just prayed about. Whichever way He reveals it to you, don't live in a state of stress. Don't live in a state of panic. It will rob you of your rest. Notice the next verse of Philippians 4, which is the result of this type of prayer. It says that the peace of God, which surpasses all understanding, will guard your heart and mind through Christ Jesus.

And now, dear brothers and sisters, one final thing. Fix your thoughts on what is true, and honorable, and right, and pure, and lovely, and admirable. Think about things that are excellent and worthy of praise. Keep putting into practice all you learned and received from me—everything you heard from me and saw me doing. Then the God of peace will be with you.

—Philippians 4:8-9 (NLT)

GUARD YOUR THOUGHTS

An unchecked thought life will rob you of your rest. Why? Every time you sit down to rest, your mind will start racing and intrusive thoughts will take over. You'll start stressing and getting anxious. You'll begin to think, "If I sit down, then who's going to do this? If I sit down, who's going to do that? What happens if this, what happens if that?"

Your mind will become consumed with all of these thoughts, all of these worries, and all of these anxieties. I wonder if Jesus looks at some of us the way He looked at Martha when He said, "Martha, Martha, you are worried and troubled about many things" (Luke 10:41 NKJV)?

Worry can rule our minds if we do not check our thought life. In order to experience the type of rest that God has for you, you will need to keep your thoughts under control. You cannot always control what thoughts pop into your head, but you can decide what you choose to think about. If you do not properly manage your thoughts, you can plan the most amazing vacation imaginable and still not rest and enjoy it. How is that possible? Changing your environment doesn't mean you automatically change your thoughts and your mindset.

Every time a thought of stress, anxiety, or worry creeps up, pray about it and then make the decision not to think about it. Say, "No, I'm not thinking about that." As my friend Pastor Kylie Gatewood teaches, you can say, "No, that is not my thought."

You cannot successfully fight thoughts with thoughts. You fight thoughts with words. Counter worrisome thoughts with Philippians 4:8 by saying, "No, I think of things that are good, lovely, just, pure, and of a good report. This is what I think."

Let's look at a story that illustrates what the spoken word can do:

Immediately Jesus made His disciples get into the boat and go before Him to the other side, while He sent the multitudes away. And when He had sent the multitudes away, He went up on the mountain by Himself to pray. Now when evening came, He was alone there. But the boat was now in the middle of the sea, tossed by the waves, for the wind was contrary.

Now in the fourth watch of the night Jesus went to them, walking on the sea. And when the disciples saw Him walking on the sea, they were troubled, saying, "It is a ghost!" And they cried out for fear.

But immediately Jesus spoke to them, saying, "Be of good cheer! It is I; do not be afraid."

And Peter answered Him and said, "Lord, if it is You, command me to come to You on the water."

So He said, "Come." And when Peter had come down out of the boat, he walked on the water to go to Jesus. But when he saw that the wind was boisterous, he was afraid; and beginning to sink he cried out, saying, "Lord, save me!"

And immediately Jesus stretched out His hand and caught him, and said to him, "O you of little faith, why did you doubt?" And when they got into the boat, the wind ceased. Then those who were in the boat came and worshiped Him, saying, "Truly You are the Son of God."

—Matthew 14:22-33 (NKJV)

In this very familiar story, we see that the wind was already boisterous. How do we know that? "The boat was now in the middle of the sea, tossed by the waves, for the wind was contrary." I want you to pay attention to the fact that the wind was already boisterous while they were in the boat.

Then, they saw Jesus walk on the water. They thought it was a ghost, and they screamed. Jesus reassured them. In so many words, He said, "Chill out guys, cheer up, be of good courage. Come on, guys, it's Me, don't be afraid."

Peter said, "If it's really You, command me to walk to You on the water."

And Jesus said, "Come on."

Follow the story with me. Peter began to walk on the water. Remember, he was looking at Jesus, he was focused on Jesus, and then he took his eyes off of Jesus. He took his focus off of Jesus and looked at the results of the wind and became afraid, and he began to sink.

Now remember, the wind was already boisterous. The wind was already contrary. The wind was already causing all the different things that were happening on that lake. Knowing this, we should understand that the wind and the waves were irrelevant. Why do I say that?

You cannot walk on the water when it is calm, and you cannot walk on the water when there is a storm. If the whole lake had been as smooth as glass in that moment, it's still water, and you still can't walk on it. The only reason Peter was able to walk on the water was because of the command of the Lord. When the Lord commanded and granted that access, he was able to walk on the result of the Word of God. It didn't matter if the wind and the waves were wild or calm, because before Jesus said it, it was impossible to do.

The wind and the waves were irrelevant. The wind was a distraction. The distraction robbed Peter of his miracle. Are distractions robbing you of your rest? Some distractions don't come from the enemy but from your own failure to plan your life; yet some distractions do come from the enemy. Either way, are distractions robbing you of your rest?

You plan to rest or take a day off and then something happens. You respond, "Oh, I have to deal with this."

Whoa, whoa, whoa. Do you?

Now, I understand that sometimes emergencies happen. Life happens, and there are things you have to handle. If that's the case, you handle it and then get back to your rest as soon as you can. Some things are, in fact, urgent. Deal with those. But there is a question you need to consider as you approach an urgent situation. Is it something that *must* be dealt with right now?

Don't automatically reply with, "I have to handle this because if I don't do it, then who will?" Stop and really think about it. Is it something that has to be done today? Is it something you can delegate? Is it something that can wait to another day at an appropriate time to handle it? Why does it have to be done right now? Answer those questions.

Not every urgency is an emergency. If you let urgency rule your life, then you'll never enjoy living. There will always be things that are urgent. Sometimes the urgent things aren't the important things. Not everything urgent is more important than your schedule, your plan, or your rest. Also, please understand that not everything in the world needs to be dealt with by you.

- Why does it need to be dealt with right now?
- Am I really the person who needs to deal with it?

Stop and take time to answer these questions. If you're constantly dealing with something urgent, you will constantly be distracted and worried about many things. On top of that, if you hear yourself saying, "Every time I take a rest, every time I go on vacation, something happens and then I am not able to rest," you are granting permission for more things along those lines to happen.

Do not let the enemy rob you of your rest. He will try to stir up problems, so you need to use the authority you have been given in the name of Jesus. According to James 1:4-6, you will also need to pray for wisdom. It takes the wisdom of the Spirit to know when to handle, what to handle, and how to handle urgent things. You have to learn to delegate things to someone else when appropriate. You also have to understand that some things need to wait until another day.

Don't live by urgency. Live by the leading of the Spirit of God. Don't always just live to put out fires. If you're not a firefighter, that is not your calling in life. Live by the leading of the Spirit of God. Get into the rhythm of rest for your life.

Remember, as you fulfill your call, God has planned times of rest for you. Do you know how I know that? Jesus, as a Jewish man under the old covenant, kept the Sabbath. He lived on earth for a little bit over 33 years. Think about that. Jesus had only 33 years to complete His mission. He only spent three years actually in ministry. Yet every week, He kept the Sabbath. Every week, He rested. He would even take time to get away, not just all night to pray, but He even took His disciples with Him one time to get away from all the busyness and pressures of ministry so that they could rest and be refreshed (see Mark 6:30-32). There's even evidence He took other breaks as well.

That sounds contrary to how we are culturally trained to think. You might have always thought, "He was the Messiah. He had three years to preach and heal, with no off days." The Messiah, the Son of God and Son of Man, took off days and took vacations—and think about all that Jesus fulfilled!

In the plan of God, the plan of the Spirit, there is rest planned. If you never take time to rest, you have left work and have crossed over to toiling. We mentioned this before, but we'll go into more detail in the next chapter.

REFLECTION QUESTIONS

We covered a lot in this chapter. Take some time to answer these questions and write down your answers in your journal.

1. What is rhythm?
2. In paying attention to yourself and how you operate, how often do you need to go somewhere? How often do you need to change the scenery? How often do you need to go to the mountains? How often do you need to go to the beach? How often do you need to go to the city? How often do you need to have an adventure?
3. Are you operating in meekness? Where do you struggle to operate in meekness?
4. What is true humility?

5. How is the rhythm of rest a partnership with the Lord of the Sabbath?

6. Is there an area in your life where you need to use your authority to stop the enemy's pattern of interference?

7. What is an intrusive thought pattern that tries to interfere with your times of rest and your ability to rest?

8. How will you determine what is urgent, what needs to be dealt with immediately, what can be delegated, and what you decide to deal with on another day?

9. How do you plan to implement what you learned in this chapter?

A PRAYER TO CONTINUALLY PRAY TO TAKE CONTROL OF YOUR THOUGHT LIFE

Father, thank You for loving me so much that You have peace for my heart and mind! I cast every care and worry upon You because You care for me. I refuse to worry. I refuse to allow intrusive thoughts to dominate my mind. According to Philippians 4:6-8, I chose to only think on what is true, and honorable, and right, and pure, and lovely, and admirable. I think about things that are excellent and worthy of praise. As a result, Your peace guards my heart and mind. Father, thank You for this. In Jesus' Name, amen.

CHAPTER 5

ARE YOU WORKING OR TOILING?

It is vain for you to rise up early, to sit up late, to eat the bread of sorrows; for so He gives His beloved sleep.

—Psalm 127:2 (NKJV)

The "bread of sorrows" is anything earned by painful toil and hardship. Toil is not work, as we discussed before. Sadly, whether they use that word or not, many people have a toil mindset. The mindset of toiling is, "I'm just going to hustle, I'm going to do all these things, I'm going to get all this money, I'm going to secure the nest egg, and then I'm going to stop."

Sadly, by the time that person stops, they have so many health issues that they have to spend "the nest egg" to recover. Or they have to spend "the nest egg" on therapy to keep their family together because they sacrificed family time for toil. What happened?

Everything they earned became nothing. Toil will lead to nothing. Why work like that all your life and get to the end of your life and have nothing to show for it? A busy life does not equal a fruitful life. Toil is not work. You are called to work, not toil. Toiling will keep you busy while working will make you fruitful. In John 15:16, Jesus said that He wanted us to be fruitful and wanted our fruit to remain. If you live by toiling, what fruit you bear will become nothing.

So God created man in His own image; in the image of God He created him; male and female He created them. Then God blessed them, and God said to them, "Be fruitful and multiply; fill the earth and subdue it; have dominion over the fish of the sea, over the birds of the air, and over every living thing that moves on the earth."

—Genesis 1:27–28 (NKJV)

Then the Lord God took the man and put him in the garden of Eden to tend and keep it.

—Genesis 2:15 (NKJV)

Then to Adam He said, "Because you have heeded the voice of your wife, and have eaten from the tree of which I commanded you, saying, 'You shall not eat of it': Cursed is the ground for your sake; in toil you shall eat of it all the days of your life. Both thorns and this-tles it shall bring forth for you, and you shall eat the herb of the field. In the sweat of your face you shall eat bread till you return to the ground, for out of it you were taken; for dust you are, and to dust you shall return."

—Genesis 3:17-19 (NKJV)

In the Garden of Eden, before sin, God gave Adam and Eve a job. He anointed them and blessed them to work. Toil was never mentioned until the curse. You're supposed to work under the blessing. Yes, work hard. Yes, work smart. Work God's way. But *work*—do not toil. If you never rest or have time to rest, I submit to you that you've entered into toil.

> The blessing of the Lord makes one rich, and He adds no sorrow with it.
>
> —Proverbs 10:22 (NKJV)

Once again, the word *sorrow* refers to painful toil and hardship. God has a way of enriching you and prospering you without toil. The way of God includes work, but it does not include toil. There's a way for you to work hard and work smart in the rhythm of rest and actually enjoy your life and prosper as you do it.

I'm not just referring to prospering financially, but prospering in every way. Your mind prospers, your emotions prosper, your relationships prosper, your family prospers, and your finances prosper. You're going to miss out on all this if you don't get into the rhythm of rest. It is useless and vain for you to work so hard from early morning until late at night, anxiously working for food to eat, for God gives rest to His loved ones. Living and working that way will lead to all you work for becoming nothing.

Once again, a rhythm is a strong, regular, repeated pattern of movement or song. I remember a song that came out over ten years ago by some very popular artists. In the song they talk about how they've made it to the top of their industry, the top of their game, but they have so many scars. That's not what God has for you. God wants to take you places in such a way that people won't be able to tell what you've been through. He doesn't want life to wear you out so you look decades older than you are! He wants your youth to be renewed (Isaiah 43:2-3). He wants people to look at you and wonder how they can live the way you are living. That's a testimony that allows you to win people to Jesus. However, if you keep toiling, your body will break down faster because your body was not made for toil—it was made for work.

Psalm 127:2 says that He gives rest to His loved ones. Don't think, "I have to earn this rest from God." No, He gives it to you because He loves you.

In order to experience this rest, you just have to get into the rhythm. Too many people are living off beat. Just because you can clap on beat doesn't mean you are living on beat.

FAITH VS. FEAR

A lot of people work out of fear because they lack faith. That lack of faith causes them to toil when they should be resting. Do you work because of fear?

Fear does not mean fright. Fear is a method of living. It is a system of operation. Sometimes it's spurred by a fright that happened to you decades ago.

I was talking to some men at the barber shop recently. I said, "If you're waking up in the morning to go to work out of fear, everything you work for will disappear."

One said, "I'm not afraid of anything. I'm strong."

He may think so now, but was he afraid of something when he was five or seven? Did something frightening happen in his childhood? Most of us do have something like that. In response to that fear, he is now saying, "I'm never going to experience that again." That choice determines his strategy of living. That's what fear does. If you are living and working out of fear, all your efforts will become nothing, because fear opens the door to the enemy to come in and destroy everything you have.

What does it look like to work out of faith? What is that mentality? It's a belief system that says, "As I wake up and I go to work today, God's going to bless the work of my hands. I believe that even if I make a mistake, His grace is going to cause it to prosper. I believe that no matter what happens in the economy, no matter what happens in my industry, no matter what happens in this nation, God's got me. Even if, for some reason, I have to switch careers to a new industry that I didn't go to school for and never learned anything about, I can prosper like Daniel because I'm anointed and God has placed me there." Now that's working out of faith, not out of fear!

Don't go to work out of fear. Go in faith, believing that you are the blessed, believing that you have favor, believing that God will open doors for you that no man can close, believing that you're called for such a time as this, believing that you have a purpose, believing that you have grace, believing that your gifts are backed with supernatural power. Don't work out of fear—work out of faith, because your expectation is in God and you believe that no matter what situation you find yourself in, God is good so you know you're going to be good.

Yes, work may look messy. You may have challenging coworkers. There could literally be crazy people around you. Have you ever considered that might be why you're there? God may have positioned you in a crazy workplace to be the light, to be the sign, to be the wonder, and to give people an opportunity to see Jesus.

RESTING IN FAITH

Your work environment does not need to be perfect in order for your gift to flourish. According to Proverbs 18:16, your gift makes room for you. Your gift opens doors. Your gift shines light. Where is light needed? In the darkness.

You shouldn't compartmentalize your God-given gift and say, "My gift only works in this area." Your gift has to work in every area. What if Dr. Martin Luther King, Jr. only used his gift inside the church? He had a great speaking gift, didn't he? He could have kept it in one spot. But he took it out of the church house. Your gift is meant for the church house, for your house, for your career, for the community. We have to learn to use our gifts in every area of life.

Your gift matters. Your gift will become more effective as you get into the rhythm of rest. You'll become more creative and realize that your rest is a declaration of faith.

Under the old covenant, when the Israelites decided they were not working on the Sabbath, they were declaring their faith. When they obeyed God and decided to let the land rest, they were declaring that they believed God would meet their needs. In the same way, when you actually sit down and rest, you're saying, "You know what? I've worked. I've done what God told me to do. Now, I'm going to rest and enjoy the fruit of my labor. Even though I'm not working today, God will still meet my needs."

Your rest is a declaration of faith. Many people don't rest because they are afraid. They say, "If I don't work, this, this, this, and this might happen." As a result, their work and career are based in fear. When something is based in fear, it's an open door for the enemy to enter and steal. Instead, you need to go to work in faith, believing that God has called you, that you are at your job for a reason, and that you are making a difference.

Fear cannot be the motive for your work. Fear cannot be the driver in your life. Why? It will destroy you. Fear will cause you to overlook your one day wins.

If you work out of fear, every time there's a hiccup in the market, you will be anxious. Every time your boss walks by your desk, you will be anxious. If you let fear motivate how you work, it won't be too long before you have panic attacks and find yourself in a constant state of anxiety.

Yes, you should have a strong work ethic, but you have to learn how to take a break and get into the rhythm of rest. Work hard, but then rest and place your faith and trust in God and His ability to take care of you. Once you learn how you rest, protect that time, because rest is holy. It will help you fulfill the plan of God for your life. Without it, your life will be cut short and you may not fulfill everything God wants you to do.

A DAILY PRAYER TO PRAY FOR YOUR BOSS, COWORKERS, AND WORK ENVIRONMENT

Father, I pray for all of those I work with. I ask that You help them, grant them wisdom, and minister peace to their hearts and minds. I ask that You help me to be light and salt in this workplace. I ask that You bless this place and cause it to increase. I speak Your peace to the atmosphere of this place and I pray that Your peace fills the entire place. I bind the plans of the enemy where this place is concerned. I pray that Your plan for this place comes to pass. According to Psalm 5:12, I ask for Your favor to surround me as a shield. Thank

You for Your help, wisdom, peace, protection, and favor.
In Jesus' Name, amen.

HOLY BY DESIGN

First Corinthians 6 says that your body is the temple of the Holy Spirit. Are you taking care of the temple of God? Part of taking care of your temple is actually resting. You're not supposed to rest only when you're exhausted. Exhaustion should not be your signal to rest.

How do I know that? God created everything in six days, and on the seventh day, He rested. Was God exhausted? No, He was *finished*. He set the example. He worked when it was time to work, and when it was time to rest, He rested. You're need to learn how to stop working when it's time to rest. You may need to cut some things off. Don't say, "Oh, I didn't finish everything. What if I don't do this?"

Well, what if you don't do it? Too many people live in a constant state of "what if" and still never get anything done. You can't live in panic. You can't live in fear. With some things, you have to learn to just wait until the next day. Perhaps there are many more things that can wait than you think.

Remember, do not now allow disorganization to rob you of rest. Some people do not rest because they are not organized. Organization means knowing which things really *must* get done today and taking care of those first. First things first! Then, at the end of the day, if there are things you didn't get done, they really can wait until tomorrow.

What is causing you to live disorganized? You may say, "Well, I'm not really good at organization." However, you probably know somebody who is— someone who finds disorder troublesome and excels in bringing organization to complete messes. It's their gift. Ask them to help you. You may not enjoy their help, but they can help you. You might say, "Oh, that doesn't sound like faith." Yes, it is. It's part of the rhythm of rest. Organize your life.

When you are disorganized, you will not be able to plan to rest. When you don't plan to rest, you won't rest. As a result, your body will enter into a forced rest, even though you had great intentions.

Do you know what I find extremely interesting when I read about rest in the Old Testament? It's called holy (Leviticus 23:3). What does it mean to be holy? It means to be set apart. When we treat rest as common, we don't rest.

We get in trouble when we make holy things common. We miss out on the adventure God has for us when we don't invite the holy into our common. We have to learn to rest by inviting the holy into our common.

Here's my question for you. Which is holier—stretching in the morning or drinking your coffee or tea? Which is holier? It's a trick question. Neither is holy in and of itself. But do you know what would make drinking coffee or stretching in the morning holy? Inviting the holy into it.

Here's something I learned from Rev. Marilyn Hickey. She's really strong on confessing the Word of God and faith-building affirmations. She shared with me that she does her faith confessions while she has her morning coffee. She has invited the holy into something common. Now her time of drinking her coffee is holy. I have even heard of people who pray wonderful prayers while they wait for their coffee to be made.

While you're stretching in the morning and you're doing the things you're supposed to do, you can take that time to talk to God and remind yourself of the promises of God. Now your routine has become holy. The holy has invaded your common.

What happens when the holy invades your common? You have opened the door for God to do amazing things in your life because you didn't keep God in your "prayer closet" or just Sunday morning. You are empowered by the Holy Spirit at all times of the day. You don't have to be this super deep Christian waiting for goose bumps to know God is there. You're living in a relationship knowing that He's with you, whether you feel Him or not, because you've invited the holy into your common.

This is a rhythm—inviting Him into your coffee time. Inviting Him into your stretching time. Inviting Him into your commute so you don't lose it on the highway. Inviting the holy into your common is another one day win worth celebrating. And the way you enter this rhythm and invite the holy into your common is by *aiming*.

REFLECTION QUESTIONS

We covered important truths in this chapter that you need to consider further. Take some time to answer the following questions in your journal.

1. Are you toiling?
2. Is your life disorganized?
3. What does it mean for rest to be holy?
4. How is rest taking care of God's temple?
5. How do you plan to invite the holy into your common?
6. Are you working out of fear?
7. How will you work out of faith?
8. What stood out the most to you in this chapter?

A PRAYER FOR YOU TO PRAY

Father, thank You for loving me. I pray that You show me where I am working and where I am toiling. Help

me to not toil, but to work under Your grace and bless-
ing. Help me to work from faith and love and not
fear. Thank You for caring about the details of my life
and for helping me to enter into the rhythm of rest. In
Jesus' Name, amen.

CHAPTER 6

A.I.M.

If you're going to invite the holy into your common and live in the rhythm of rest, you will need aim. You need to have good aim, on the level of the fictional character Robin Hood. How do you aim, and what do I mean by aiming? Invite the holy into your common through Acknowledging, Inquiring, and Meditation.

ACKNOWLEDGE

Trust in the Lord with all your heart, and lean not on your own understanding; *in all your ways acknowledge Him*, and He shall direct your paths.

—Proverbs 3:5-6 (NKJV)

You have many different "ways" you deal with every day, right? You have work-related ways, family-related ways, finance-related ways. You have several things you have to deal with. However, when you acknowledge Him, He will direct you. What does the word *acknowledge* mean? It means to recognize Him.

Now, you don't have to start your day praying, "God, be with me today." Why? He's already with you. If you're born again, He's on the inside of you. If you're baptized in the Holy Spirit, He's resting upon you. Also, He dwells in your midst.

If you pray, "Oh, God, be with me today," He says, "I got that covered. I'm already with you."

If you pray for God to be with you, you don't really believe He's already with you—you believe He's far away. But He's not far away from you. First Corinthians 6 says that you, believer, are one spirit with the risen Christ. He's closer to you than your breath.

Instead of praying for God to be with you, you should say, "Father, thank You for being with me."

What is that? That's recognizing Him. The more you say, "Thank You for being with me," the more aware you become of His presence. The more aware you become of Him, the more you realize that He's there even when you don't feel "spiritual goose bumps." You know He's there because you are recognizing Him.

In all your ways acknowledge Him—recognize Him. Another word for this is to *know Him*. Know Him in all your ways. Know what He would want you to do. Know what He thinks about it. We shouldn't only know Him in spiritual things. Some people are really good asking God about spiritual things. Ask Him about everything. Talk to Him about everything. Recognize Him in everything. As you do that, your aim will grow increasingly better.

INQUIRE

One of the things that is so interesting to me in the Books of Judges, 1 Samuel, and 2 Samuel is how often they inquired of the Lord and how often they did not. First Samuel says:

Then David inquired of the Lord once again. And the Lord answered him and said, "Arise, go down to Keilah. For I will deliver the Philistines into your hand."

—1 Samuel 23:4 (NKJV)

David had inquired once before and then he did it again. Now, there are times in David's life when he didn't inquire at all. Other times, he inquired repeatedly. Every time the people of God inquired multiple times, they received more information each time.

Inquire means more than simply "to ask," as in a request. People think they are inquiring when they ask for something. No, inquiring means you're seeking information or God's will in a matter. When you inquire of God, you receive information from Him.

Some of us get so excited when we hear God speak to us. We rejoice and run off, saying, "God talked to me." Of course God talked to you. He likes to talk to you. But before you run off, make sure you got everything. In a lot of things, we receive partial information and then run off with the part we got and try to do it in our own might, our own strength, and our own way. Then, when we don't get the results we were after, we say, "Oh man, I didn't hear from God."

No, you did hear from God. You just didn't stay long enough to get the rest of the instructions. You have to inquire, and as you do it, you inquire again. When they inquired under the old covenant, they had to have a priest come out with the Urim and the Thummim, and they would go through the whole process to inquire of the Lord. You don't have to do that. You just have to ask Him and then ask again.

What does the second inquiry sound like? You ask questions such as, "What else do I need to know about this?"

You might say, "Well, God, You didn't talk to me about this." Did you ask Him about it?

You might say, "Oh, God's been talking to me about things I didn't ask for." Well, do you pray in the Holy Spirit? If you do, there are times you are asking Him about things and you just didn't know it. Sometimes, out of God's absolute mercy or because someone prayed for you and asked on your behalf, you receive vital information from God that you did not even ask for. We have to develop the spiritual habit of inquiring and inquiring again.

When you look at the lives of the judges in 1 and 2 Samuel, they were all anointed. They were heavily empowered by God. However, some of these anointed judges did not know the character of God, and that's why they made the mistakes they did. Some of them didn't inquire of God, and that's why they got the results they got.

Despite the results, they were still anointed and empowered by God. You, Christian, are anointed. But your results don't always look anointed, do they? Did you inquire? And did you inquire again?

Sometimes we get ourselves into a habit of only inquiring about "big things." Some people say, "Well, God told me to do this 30 years ago." That's great. Have you checked in since then? We're human, and in our application of God's instructions, we can miss it.

If you're flying in an airplane and you get one degree off course, eventually you end up in a completely different city. You think you are going to Atlanta, but you end up in New York. Just one degree, not checked for a period of time, can cause you to end up in the wrong city.

That can happen in your life if you don't keep inquiring and keep checking in. It's not always about falling on your knees, saying, "Oh God, am I going to the right place?" You just live life and check in with Him, asking, "Hey God, am I doing this right? Okay, You told me to go here, what's my next step?"

Sometimes He will answer you with a "Just chill." Or, "Go and do what you planned to do." Other times, He'll give you specific instructions. When you get in the habit of inquiring of Him, you'll get in the habit of hearing from Him. If you're going to enter into the rhythm of rest, you have to have new habits—the habit of acknowledging and the habit of inquiring.

MEDITATE

This Book of the Law shall not depart from your mouth, but you shall meditate in it day and night, that you may observe to do according to all that is written in it. For then you will make your way prosperous, and then you will have good success.

—Joshua 1:8 (NKJV)

In my book *No Longer Mere Mortals* I shared:

God's instructions to Joshua were clear. He was not supposed to let the book of the law depart from his mouth. In other words, he was supposed to keep saying it. The reason is simple— saying it aloud changed his mindset, showed him how to live, and built his faith. The book of the law was not just a list of commandments; this book also contained all the promises God gave concerning the promised land. The book of the law, Genesis to Deuteronomy, contained the stories of supernatural acts of God's power, provision, and deliverance. This book of the law was what Joshua needed to see, say, and hear on a regular basis in order to accomplish the superhuman feat of possessing the promised land.

The word *meditate* in verse 8 can also be translated as "to imagine, to meditate, to say, to study, to talk, to speak, to mutter, and to roar." Notice how many times it is translated in a way that means verbal communication. In the context of Joshua 1:8, we see that God fully expected Joshua to study, to meditate, and to speak. …We must always put ourselves in the position to receive faith by hearing through reading the word aloud, by hearing the anointed word preached and taught, and by hearing the Holy Spirit speak the word to our hearts.

Biblical meditation is not about getting in a quiet place and trying to come to the center of yourself. Quiet places can help us in many different ways, but that is not what biblical mediation is. Meditation is what you think about continually.

Meditation is not strange to you because you do it all the time. You just have a different word for it.

Your playlist on your phone is your meditation list. Whatever song you keep listening to is what you're meditating on. Whatever TV show you keep watching again and again—that's what you're meditating on. Whatever broadcast you continue to listen to— that's your meditation.

My question to you is: what are you meditating on right now? What you're meditating on is producing in your life. Now, I'm not saying that you can't be aware of what goes on in the world. Be aware, just don't meditate on it. Watch the news, just don't meditate on it. Be an informed voter, just don't meditate on it. Your chief meditation has to be on the Word of God.

Whether it's just reading the Word, listening to it, or putting the Word to music, your chief meditation, the number-one thing you meditate on has to be God's Word. If the Word becomes your chief meditation, you will make your way prosperous. You don't have to say, "Oh God, make my way prosperous today." Meditate on His Word and then you'll have good success (Joshua 1:8). The word for *prosperous* in this verse is *saleah*, which contains the meaning of breaking out and pushing forward—what we would call breakthrough (Strong's H6743). What is breakthrough? It's an important discovery or event that helps to improve a situation or provide an answer to a problem. A breakthrough is also a notable victory over previous limitations and hindrances.

Do you need something to break out and break through for you? Meditate on God's Word. What happens when you meditate on God's Word and you keep saying the Word of God and thinking on it? The Word begins to speak to you. When the Word begins to speak to you, you'll know what to say. It's good to just take the general Word of God and read it out loud and go through the promises of God and read those aloud. Those practices help you to renew your mind and to build your faith. But to take it to the next level, to release your faith and change things in your life, you have to let the Word speak to you and inform what you say.

Recently, I was traveling and preaching at a wonderful men's conference in Wales. In between sessions, one of the speakers, Pastor Paul Brady, kept saying a scripture from the Psalms, "The Lord is among those who help us." It jumped out to me so I clung to it.

I found that verse in the Psalms, I began to say it again and again, "The Lord is for me among those who help me" (Psalm 118:7 NKJV). When a situation would come up and we needed God to show up, I would say "The Lord is among those who help us." Then we would see wild things happen for us and things would turn in our favor. That verse was my meditation for months. As I kept saying it, I added something to it. I now say, "The Lord is among those who help us. And I expect the help of the Lord today in normal ways, surprising ways, and supernatural ways."

Where did that come from? I've been meditating on that Scripture and now it has informed my language. What's the result? I get the help of the Lord in normal ways, in surprising ways, in supernatural ways, and in open doors that I didn't even know were there. Because I meditated on it, now the Word informs what I'm saying.

Meditate on what He said and He'll tell you what to say. Very rarely is it a big, booming voice from

Heaven bellowing, "Thus saith the Lord." You get it on the inside, you become aware of it. You pick up on it in your spirit. You realize, "Oh, I need to start saying that. I need to start talking about that. I need to stop saying that."

Why? Because there are times when the Holy Spirit will check you on the inside and tell you to stop saying something. He'll tell you, "Don't make that joke. Stop saying that you're old."

There have been viral videos on TikTok and Instagram joking about being old—how much your bones pop when you get out of bed and all those things. The videos may be funny, but stop agreeing with them. You have a promise from God. He will renew your youth as the eagle's and with long life will He satisfy you and show you His salvation (see Psalms 103:5; 91:16).

A.I.M. FOR REST

In our aiming, we have to aim for rest. God doesn't just give you a place to rest, the Bible says He makes you lie down:

The Lord is my shepherd; I shall not want. He makes me to lie down in green pastures; He leads me beside the still waters.

—Psalm 23:1-2 (NKJV)

"I will feed My flock, and I will make them lie down," says the Lord God.

—Ezekiel 34:15 (NKJV)

Throughout Psalm 23, David uses the language of shepherding to show how God leads and takes care of us. "Making the sheep lie down" refers to how shepherds would rest their sheep. They would lead the sheep to a good, protected place when it was time to rest. However, sheep are very panicky. Even in a restful spot, there are certain conditions they need in order to rest and not panic. Do you know one of the chief conditions? The presence of the shepherd.

The presence of the shepherd helps the sheep lie down. The presence of the shepherd helps the sheep experience rest.

How can you experience the presence of the shepherd? By aiming—acknowledging, inquiring, and meditating. When you do these things, you'll be aware that He's with you, because all those who keep their minds stayed on Him will experience a perfect, complete, whole peace (Isaiah 26:3).

If you want to get into the rhythm of rest for your life, you're going to have to acknowledge, you're going to have to inquire, and you're going to have to meditate. These must become your new habits. If you do, you'll learn how to rest and enjoy your life. You don't need to live for a vacation. Vacations are nice. You should take them. However, you don't live for them. If a vacation is the only time when you rest and enjoy your life, you're not living the life God has for you.

Jesus, as the Good Shepherd, said, "I've come that you might have and enjoy life to the full, till it overflows" (see John 10:10 AMPC). As you aim, He'll teach you how you rest. He'll teach you how to live and live freely. You'll have rest for your body, because your body needs it. You'll have rest for your mind, because your mind needs it. You'll have rest for your emotions, because your emotions need it.

The other part of your soul is the will. Does your will need to rest too? Yes. There are so many people today who have what they call "decision burnout." They get home and say, "I can't make another decision because I made so many decisions today." The Good Shepherd even has rest for your decision burnout.

Most of all, He has rest for your spirit. We live in a chaotic world, but you don't need to have the chaos on the inside. Even in chaos, you can rest inside because God loves you. To experience that rest, you need to aim.

So many people think they won't rest until they get to Heaven. And guess what? They don't experience rest, so they're right. But one day, they will look back and realize, "Oh, God had rest for me all the time." Don't be that person. Don't be the person who waits until they retire or until their vacation to enjoy their life. Enter into that flow now. When you get into this rhythm of rest, God will grant you vacations that are beyond what you thought you could ever afford. You'll see God just give you stuff, like opportunities to vacation at your favorite resort for less than the normal cost. I regularly experience it, and you can too!

It's a rhythm. It's a pattern. It's a lifestyle. A life of favor, upgrades, and preferential treatment. It is the lifestyle of the blessed and the favored. You have favor! God's favor in the rhythm of rest will supply you with things that you could never get by working, opportunities that you didn't even know were available, and wonderful blessings that you didn't know how to resource.

Why do you have such favor? Because God loves you. What do you need to do with this favor? Acknowledge it, meditate on it, A.I.M. for it. God will show you favor in the lifestyle of the rhythm of rest. Meditate upon this. Think about how favored you are that God would simply give you something that other people might work decades for. Or, we could say it this way: God gives you what others toil decades for and still can't get. But God just gives it to you and you receive it by faith. It's yours. It's the lifestyle of faith in the rhythm of rest.

You simply say, "God told me to rest and my rest is a declaration of faith." When you make a declaration of faith, there's a response of grace. In the rhythm of rest, you're actually resting in faith and will be met by manifestations and gifts of grace.

REFLECTION QUESTIONS

Consider these questions and write down your answers in your journal.

1. What stood out to you the most in this chapter?
2. How do you plan to acknowledge and recognize the Lord in your life?
3. What are some areas in your life where you need to further inquire of the Lord?
4. How will you incorporate biblical meditation into your daily life and routine?
5. How is your rest a declaration of faith?

A PRAYER FOR YOU TO PRAY

Father, I pray that You will help me A.I.M. Help me to acknowledge You in all my ways, consistently inquire of You and further inquire of You, and meditate on Your words and promises. Help me to enter into the rhythm of rest for my life. In Jesus' Name, amen.

CHAPTER 7

OPPORTUNITIES OF REST

I have a question for you. When you do have time to rest, are you actually capitalizing on that rest? I have had the opportunity to minister along these lines in a number of different places. One time after ministering, I had the opportunity to sit down with Pastor George Pearsons. We had a wonderful conversation about a number of topics, including the rhythm of rest. In the conversation, he said, "I take every available opportunity that comes my way to rest. Even if it's just 30 minutes, I take those 30 minutes." That conversation enhanced and expanded my thinking on this subject.

You might say, "Well, 30 minutes is not a lot."

It's better than none. Let's say you get 30 minutes. What are you going to do with it? Are you going to miss the opportunity to rest because you're just scrolling on social media and getting mad at the posts, the AI, and the algorithm? Have you ever done that? You got upset, and in the end you let an algorithm steal your time to rest.

If that's an issue for you, what might you need to do to rest? Put your phone down. I've set up a "rest mode" on my phone that blocks certain notifications and rearranges my screen. If it's my time to rest, I turn on that mode so that I don't miss my opportunity to rest. When opportunities to rest come your way, are you taking advantage of them?

Even small opportunities to rest are still opportunities. Ephesians 5:16 tells us to make the most of *every* opportunity in evil or troublesome times. People always talk about the dark times we are living in. It's true, and that means we are to take advantage of every open door and opportunity God brings our way, including opportunities to rest.

The Amplified Bible says, "making the very most of your time [on earth, recognizing and taking advantage of each opportunity and using it with wisdom and diligence], because the days are [filled with] evil" (Ephesians 5:16 AMP). We are to take advantage of opportunities. This is what the phrase "redeeming the time" means in the New King James Version. It means to take advantage of opportunities.

TAKING ADVANTAGE OF OPPORTUNITIES

If you are going to "redeem the time," you must think like a savvy shopper who always scores the best deals. They go to stores and search online with a certain mindset. What are they intensely looking for? The best deals. We have to approach our opportunities with that mindset. When God brings open doors our way, we must take advantage of them like a savvy shopper would take advantage of the best deal.

Part of being a savvy shopper is being able to recognize the good deal when it arrives. When the Lord gives you opportunities to rest, as the Scriptures say He will, do you recognize those opportunities? Or do you miss the best deal because you were looking for something different? Are you turning down opportunities to rest?

You might say, "Well, it's not a two-week vacation."

I didn't say it will always be a two-week vacation, I said *opportunities*. Sometimes you get 15 minutes. Sometimes you get 30 minutes. Sometimes you get half a day. Sometimes you get an opportunity to go on a vacation. When God brings these opportunities your way, are you recognizing them as your time to rest and taking advantage of them?

Peace and rest are blessings. God always brings you these opportunities—don't spoil them because of a lack of faith, discipline, planning, vision, or self-control. Take advantage of the opportunities God brings your way to rest, even if it's just 15 minutes, 30 minutes, or an hour. Do you know what happens if you take advantage of your opportunities to rest at all those increments? You get into the rhythm of rest.

STRIVING VS. SELAH

God opens doors for you that no man can close. He brings open doors for you to be supernaturally productive and get things done, but He also brings opportunities your way to rest. Are you trying to work through those opportunities? Are you spoiling them by not guarding your thought life? Are you allowing your emotions to run amok instead of operating in meekness and following the leading of God's Spirit?

Remember, a lack of faith, planning, discipline, vision, and self-control will cause you to toil when you should be resting and enjoying the fruit of your labor. Toiling can destroy your health because of the diet choices you make when you're in a rush. If you're toiling, you won't take the time to eat what you should eat and you'll just eat whatever is put in front of you. You'll consume unhealthy things that are technically not even food. In order to stop toiling and live in the rhythm of rest, we have to learn how to stop striving and be still.

> *Stop striving* and know that I am God; I will be exalted among the nations, I will be exalted on the earth.
>
> —Psalm 46:10 (NASB)

"Stop striving" in the New King James Version is translated "be still." It means to let go and relax. How often are you actually still? Not just still physically, but still mentally and emotionally? How often do you actually take a step back to just chill and say, "He's God. He's got this."

This is part of the rhythm. There's another word for it in Psalms. It's *selah*, which means to pause and think about the verse at hand.

Lord, how they are increased who trouble me! Many are they who rise up against me. Many are saying of me, There is no help for him in God. ***Selah [pause, and calmly think of that]***! But You, O Lord, are a shield for me, my glory, and the lifter of my head. With my voice I cry to the Lord, and He hears and answers me out of His holy hill. ***Selah [pause, and calmly think of that]***! I lay down and slept; I wakened again, for the Lord sustains me. I will not be afraid of ten thousands of people who have set themselves against me round about.

—Psalm 3:1-6 (AMPC)

Part of the rhythm of rest is taking time to selah—pause and think. When you get into the rhythm of rest and you take time to pause and be still, you're able to reflect. How many times do we do the same thing incorrectly again and again and again because we never reflect? We live so fast paced that we never take time to stop and think. We don't take the time to ask ourselves, "Hey, did that work out? Did that actually have the impact I want?"

When was the last time you paused to reflect? Being still in the presence of God, knowing He's God, you are able reflect over your week. You are able to ask yourself, "Do I need to make an adjustment in the upcoming week?"

When you take time to reflect, you are also able to realize, "Wow, God did some amazing stuff this week." How many times do we miss the miracle because we don't stop to reflect? We don't realize what God did because we didn't stop long enough to see what He did. Could we possibly be ungrateful because we never stopped to reflect and give God thanks for what He did for us?

When was the last time you paused, outside of church, and thought about what He did for you and where He brought you from? It's so easy to get caught up in the trouble of the moment and forget about the 30,000 times He's delivered you in the past.

How often have you wondered, "I don't know how I'm going to make it through this?" But whoa, wait. Isn't that what you said five years ago? Ten years ago? Fifteen years ago? Yet here you are.

You'll miss God's track record of faithfulness if you never stop and realize, "I've come a long way. I may not be where I want to be, but I'm not where I used to be, and I'm not *who* I used to be." You won't see that unless you stop, selah, pause, and think about it.

There are many things you can do to accomplish this part of the rhythm of rest. You can make a habit of journaling. You can just take a regular walk in nature and thank God for what He did for you that week. Whichever way you choose, make it a time to pause and reflect and think. This will remind you of God's faithfulness, which will bring rest to you, help you become more creative, and help you think on a higher level.

When you selah, you are able to realize your one day wins. The rhythm of rest calls for times to selah. It calls for times to pause. When you pause and rest, you are able to reflect, and when you reflect you are able to perceive.

WHAT DO YOU PERCEIVE?

In Old Testament, the prophet Isaiah talks about people who see but don't perceive: "Keep on hearing, but do not understand; keep on seeing, but do not perceive" (Isaiah 6:9 NKJV). In the New Testament, Jesus quotes this verse in both Matthew and Mark, and Paul quotes it in the Book of Acts. This concept is clearly important in both an old and new covenant context. There are people who can look right at something but they can't *perceive* it. What does this mean? The word *perceive* means to become deeply aware of something.

When was the last time you perceived something? I actually believe you perceive things all the time, but you don't stop long enough to realize that you perceived something.

The perceiving I'm talking about does not come from your mind, reason, feelings, or five physical senses. Yes, you should know the thoughts in your head. You should know how your body feels. You should pay attention to these different voices. However, I'm not referring to perceiving with your senses or your mind. I'm referring to perceiving with your spirit.

You have to realize that your spirit picks up on things. You are a three-part being. You are a spirit, you have a soul (which is your mind, your will, and the control center of your emotions), and you live in a physical body. If your body and soul can pick up on things, your spirit can also pick up on things. If you don't take the time to pause and reflect, you'll miss those perceptions. And if you don't write them down, you will forget them.

And David perceived that the Lord had established him king over Israel, and that he had exalted his kingdom for his people Israel's sake.

—2 Samuel 5:12 (KJV)

In this verse, David had finally been anointed king. Several things had transpired on his journey to becoming king over all of Israel. It was a long journey. After he was officially in place, all of a sudden he became aware: "Woah! The Lord has established me. He's exalted my kingdom for His people's sake!"

Have you ever had a sudden "aha" moment like this, when you became aware of something God was doing in your life? You had a sudden moment of clarity. However, life came at you fast. You didn't pause and reflect, and as result you never did anything with the revelation or clarity your spirit perceived. What have you forgotten because you didn't pause?

You pick up on things all the time. It's not always a voice. Sometimes it's just a knowing, as if you become aware on the inside and you say, "Oh, I got it."

Here's a pro tip for your prayer life: take what you perceive to prayer. Should we pray about our thoughts? Sure. Should we pray about our feelings? Sure. But if you want to advance in the call of God on your life, you need to take what you perceive to prayer. When you do, you'll realize, "Oh, this is what God is doing in my life." There will be faith for the impossible because you're picking things up from the Spirit of God.

YOU AND THE SPIRIT

A lot of times people miss their chance to use their faith because they copy other faith giants. It is good and scriptural to do that sometimes. Hebrews 6:12 teaches us to be followers of those who through faith and patience inherit the promises. What should we follow or imitate? Their *faith* and *patience*.

But have you ever tried to directly copy the *method* of a spiritual person you admire? Sometimes it works for you, but then other times it's clearly not working at all. Why didn't a good, solid, spiritual method work for you in those times? The reason it worked for them and not for you is because they heard from the Holy Ghost and did what He told them to do. However, you're trying to do what He told *them* to do, and it's not working for you.

Faith still works, but you're going to have to perceive something on the inside and realize, "Oh, that's what I'm supposed to do." Then after you become aware of what you are supposed to do, further inquire of the Lord by asking, "What more do I need to know about this?"

As you read 1 Samuel and 2 Samuel, you'll see how often they inquired of the Lord. Sometimes they inquired of the Lord, and other times they didn't. Sometimes, God gave one answer, but when they stayed before Him they received even more. Remember that the "I" in A.I.M. stands for *inquire*. After you perceive something, take time to inquire and talk to God about it. When you take what you receive to prayer, you're setting yourself up for impossible things to become possible.

And said unto them, Sirs, I perceive that this voyage will be with hurt and much damage, not only of the lading and ship, but also of our lives.

—Acts 27:10 (KJV)

In Acts, Paul was on this boat and he became aware that this journey was not going to turn out the way they wanted it to. The Scripture does not say an angel spoke to him. It does not say he had a vision. It says he *perceived*. All of a sudden, he became aware, "This is not right." And if they had followed Paul's perception, all of their cargo would have been saved.

How many times have you suffered loss because you didn't follow what you perceived, maybe because it didn't seem to make sense? It's very simple. Believers and non-believers alike experience this. They say, "Something just told me." It wasn't a something, but a Someone—the Holy Spirit.

If non-believers can pick up on things, shouldn't you as a saint of the Most High God? You might pick up on things when you're in church. God will start talking to you about something that has nothing to do with what the minister is sharing. Take notes on the message and also on what God speaks to your heart. Write it down so you don't forget it. Then take it to Him in prayer and inquire about it.

This isn't about your reasoning. It's not about your logic. Some people call it a feeling, but it's not really your emotions. It's becoming aware on the inside, because you are a spirit. Perceiving things does not mean you're spooky. The Holy Ghost is not spooky. Spooky, weird people make the Holy Ghost seem spooky and weird. The Holy Ghost is not like that. He's the One who's setting the rhythm for your rest. If you get into this rhythm, you'll be more supernatural. You'll have more supernatural results, and you will enjoy your life.

Remember to take what you perceive to prayer. As you get into this rhythm, or you can call it "God's flow," you pick up on more. You won't only pick up on things during "super deep" times, but also in your everyday life. Why? You're inviting the holy into your common, remember? As a result, you will pick up things from Him even in the common parts of life.

We are made to live this way. Many times, we're waiting for some goose bumps before we try to make a difference in our world or in a situation. What happens if you find yourself in a place where people need your help but you don't feel "spiritual" that day? Do you tell them to try again tomorrow? They don't know God, but they need an answer from God and they look at you. Jesus said that you are the salt and the light of this earth, so God will give you an answer. Well, where's the answer? On the inside.

ACCESSING THE TREASURE HOUSE

I remember years ago when I was still a teenager being trained in ministry. The person who was training me was taking me around to different places to teach me about the elements of pastoral care. After church one day, the minister was praying for people. As he was praying over this couple, he stopped, looked at me, and said, "Hey, do you have something?"

I was like, "Do I have something? Wait, do I have something?" I didn't know. I paused and closed my eyes. I can only explain it as I looked on the inside of my heart, and it was like I reached down and I grabbed something. Then all of a sudden, out of my mouth I began to prophesy over this couple. I was a teenager prophesying over them. Before I knew it,

I reached out and laid hands on them, and they flew backward under the power of the Spirit. The minister training me had to catch me because I almost went with them.

Where did that come from? On the inside. There's more on the inside of you than you realize. There's more to you than meets the eye. Your spirit, Jesus says, is a treasure house. It's a storehouse (Matthew 12:35). God has put those things inside of you for this time. You're here for such a time as this. God has gifted you, equipped you, anointed you, and empowered you with everything you need to make a difference in this present time.

If you want to make a difference that lasts, you need to get into the rhythm of rest. You need to take time to pause and reflect and perceive. If you do, not only will you be the light and salt, you'll enjoy the life Jesus has for you. What does it say in John 10:10?

The thief comes only in order to steal and kill and destroy. I came that they may have and enjoy life, and have it in abundance (to the full, till it overflows).

—John 10:10 (AMPC)

It's time to make a difference and have fun while we do it. Rest, reflect, perceive. You really can hear from God. You may not think you can, but Jesus said you could. In John 10:27 (KJV), He said, "My sheep hear my voice, and I know them, and they follow me."

Stop telling yourself you can't hear from God. Sit down, be still, and stop striving. What are you picking up on? He'll talk to you, and He'll talk to you in a way that you understand.

Don't think He'll only talk to you using King James English. Unless you normally speak like the King James Version, He's not going to talk to you in that old English. Don't expect *thus saith* and *thou art*. That's not what He's going to do. He knows you. He knows what grabs your attention. You might sit there and hear the Holy Ghost say, "Bruh."

You'll think, "Where did that come from? Did the Holy Ghost just say, 'Bruh'?" There's a whole bunch of Gen Z lingo God might use to speak to Gen Z because that's the way they talk. He will speak to you in a way that you understand.

Don't try to make it so deep and difficult. Just chill out and hear from the Holy Ghost who loves you. He's not far away. He's closer to you than your breath. He lives on the inside of you.

A HIGHER WAY OF LIVING

On LinkedIn, I post a lot of different business and corporate articles, devotionals, and other resources to help people in their careers. And as I was on LinkedIn, I saw another creator share about people who live for vacation. Fifty weeks out of the year are horrible for them, but two weeks of the year are good for them. They live for that vacation.

Living for vacation is not a good way to live. That is not the way God has for you. Do you think that God only wants you to enjoy two weeks out of your fifty-two? That's a low level of living. Do you think God wants you to only enjoy your life when you retire? That's how some people approach their careers: "I'm going to do this, I'm going to do this, I'm going to hustle and do all this. And then when I retire, I can finally live my life."

A lot of people live this way, but don't you think God has something better for you? I submit to you that if you only start to enjoy your life after you retire, that's still a low level of living. The rhythm of rest is a higher way of living.

> "For My thoughts are not your thoughts, nor are your ways My ways," says the Lord. "For as the heavens are higher than the earth, so are My ways higher than your ways, and My thoughts than your thoughts."
>
> —Isaiah 55:8–9 (NKJV)

God's ways are higher than your ways, and His rhythm is higher, too. To enter into the rhythm of rest for your life, you have to live in a higher way.

Recently, I was in Michigan vising with my family. That Saturday I went to the gym with my brothers. One of my brothers was helping me perfect my deadlift, showing me how to do it right and making sure I was lifting correctly.

While we were working out, he said, "The way you're lifting, you're going against the flow of your body. Whenever you go against the flow of your body, you will be injured. But when you go with the flow, you'll be good." He said, "It's just like the Holy Ghost. When you go with His flow, you're good. When you don't, you'll be in trouble." He then smiled and told me that I could add that into one of my messages. I did, and I have included it in this book because there's so much truth in that. When we go against the flow of the Holy Spirit, we find ourselves in trouble. We find ourselves in problems and issues and situations, saying, "I don't know how I got myself into this." You went against the flow. There is a flow of rest for you. There's a rhythm of rest. There's a time to work and there's a time to rest.

REFLECTION QUESTIONS

Consider these questions and write down your answers in your journal.

1. Do you take advantage of opportunities to rest? If you do not, what causes you not to?
2. How often do you take time to be still and reflect?
3. How do you implement what you learn through reflection into your everyday life?
4. What does it mean to perceive?
5. What are you currently perceiving about your life?
6. What are your one day wins for today?

A PRAYER FOR YOU TO PRAY

Father, I thank You that You sent the Holy Spirit to lead and guide me into all truth. I ask that You help me to become even more sensitive to His leadings. Help me to act upon what I perceive and to be diligent enough to follow up and inquire even more of You. Grant me ears to hear, eyes to see, and a heart to perceive Your guidance in my life. I thank You for all of these things. In Jesus' Name, amen.

CHAPTER 8

WHAT'S INTERFERING WITH YOUR REST?

Learning how you rest means paying attention to yourself. You are a three-part being. You are a spirit, you have a soul (which is your mind, will, and control center of your emotions), and you live in a physical body. You have to pay attention to your entire being, including listening to your body.

You may say, "Oh, I don't listen to my body." You actually listen to your body all the time. If your body tells you that you're hungry, what do you do? You go get something to eat. Now, if you let your body lead the way, you'll eat more than you should, or you'll eat things you shouldn't. So you should listen to the voice of your body, but you need to keep your body in check with the voice of your spirit. Why?

Because your spirit is born again. The Holy Ghost lives in your spirit, and that makes your spirit a safe guide. Since you are a believer, you can always let your conscience be your guide. Jiminy Cricket got that one right. If you're born again, your conscience is a safe guide because it is picking up and perceiving things from the Spirit of God. Your body will let you know what you're feeling right now, but you make the decision to put your body in its place.

Sometimes your body says, "I need to eat," and you actually do need to go eat. Sometimes your body says, "I need to go rest," and you actually do need to go rest. Some people think that when they ignore the voice of their body they are operating in faith. Faith is not necessarily ignoring your body; it's having dominion over your body. It is the operation of the fruit of the Spirit called self-control (Galatians 5:22–23). Even in the lifestyle of faith, you have to pay attention to what your body calling for. In work, yes, you can get on the wrong side of this issue and become lazy and never work. If you do, you'll get the results of laziness that the Book of Proverbs plainly highlights and repeats in several verses and chapters. However, that's not what we are focusing on because that's not the issue at hand. The issue at hand is not actually resting.

You also have the voice of your mind, which is reason. Your mind can help you realize, "You need to back up from thinking about this and take a mental break." Now, your mind will tell you to do a lot of things. That doesn't mean it's always right. You have to keep the voice of the mind in check with the voice of your spirit.

You might say, "Well, all of that sounds complicated. How do I know if it's the Holy Spirit talking to me or my spirit or my mind or my body?"

As you study God's Word and continually put into practice the A.I.M. principles, it becomes simpler and simpler. The Holy Spirit will never tell you to do something that's against the Word of God. The voice of your spirit and the Holy Spirit in your spirit will always agree with the Word of God. When your mind tells you to do something that's against the Word, you check it, resist the thought, and renew your mind with what the Bible actually says. When your body tells you to do something that's against the Word, you check it and make a decision to do what is right instead of what you feel.

Here's a pro tip for dealing with these things. If you're having a struggle with your mind or your body, get an accountability partner. An accountability partner is someone you can honestly talk to who will remind you to stay on God's path and live the way He has called you to live.

ELIMINATING OBSTACLES TO YOUR REST

A couple of years ago, the Lord started talking to me about some things I could do to take care of my physical body that would help me enter into the rhythm of rest. In response to His instruction and to make sure I was resting and sleeping enough, I learned how to make my technology work for me. I started to track how many hours I sleep, how often I sleep, and my sleep patterns. I began to explore the concept of sleep debt in my life.

Sleep debt is a deficit in your total time spent asleep. It is basically the cumulative burden on your body from lack of sleep that builds up when you regularly miss sleep over a period of time. The amount of sleep you need changes throughout your life. However, the average adult usually needs between seven to eight hours every night.[8]

In applying what I learned, I set my screen devices to show certain lights during the day and certain lights after the sun sets. Blue light from electronic devices fools the brain into thinking that it is daytime and it keeps your mind awake. As a result, the body doesn't release the sleep hormone melatonin. This sleep hormone helps the body wind down and prepare for bed. Darkness helps trigger the release of melatonin a few hours before bedtime.[9] Since electronic blue light can delay or interrupt this process, I have changed the settings on my screens. During night hours, those blue lights aren't shining in my face, even if I'm working. This helps my mind and my body to prepare to rest.

In the same way, there are certain things you shouldn't drink or eat late at night or even in the late afternoon if you're going to rest properly. You may have been able to process caffeine well before, but now your body is saying, "Hey, I'm wired because I had coffee at 4 p.m." You have to listen to your body and make a change. Did you know that an unhealthy diet and heavy consumption of ultra-processed foods impacts a person's deep sleep and is connected to insomnia?[10]

If you have trouble getting to sleep because your mind is always racing, what can you do to put your mind to rest? For some, a focused mental activity that is different from work can be helpful. Maybe you need a journal to write down your thoughts. Maybe you need to record and process your day. Maybe you need to do a physical puzzle or a crossword puzzle. Anything that allows your mind to wind down so that you can rest.

Prepare thoroughly! For example, if you know you need to read a book or do some journaling to help you fall asleep, then don't be scrambling to find your journal, puzzle, or book you need right before you go to bed. Instead of relaxing and resting, you're searching—you haven't established a habit in the rhythm of rest. Instead, when you wake up in the morning, as a part of your morning routine, put that journal on your pillow or right next to your bed so that it's ready for you when you go to lie down at night. Now, you don't have to look for it. You have set yourself up for success and are working toward establishing a good habit.

CHANGING HABITS

Although we're redeemed from the curse of the law (Galatians 3:13), although we've come into the body of Christ and we're redeemed from so many different things, we still have to change our habits. Redemption means that Jesus bought us back from the curse and the control of the enemy—it *doesn't* mean that all of your bad habits disappeared. We need to change our habits to line up with the lifestyle God has called us to live. A person may be saved, sanctified, filled with the Holy Ghost, and going to Heaven, but that does not mean that person has learned to work under the blessing in the rhythm of rest. If we haven't changed our habits, we may still be working and toiling like those in the world. Remember, toil was introduced in the Fall. You are called to work hard and smart under the blessing, but God has not called you to toil. You are redeemed from toiling.

Paying attention to yourself helps you eliminate simple obstacles to your rest. There are habits you need to look at and examine in your life. There are some natural habits and some spiritual habits. Rest is more than just sleep—you need to continually learn what is rest for you. It's a process.

Think about musicians. When a musician first starts playing, even if they're one of those superbly talented people who can learn very quickly, most of them don't get everything right. They'll hit a few bad notes. They may get out of rhythm; they may get off tempo. But as they practice, they learn stay in the rhythm. They can keep the tempo. They can play the right notes. It's the same here—as you apply the principles of this book, you're getting into the rhythm of rest. Don't be discouraged just because you got off beat and played the wrong note. Get back into the rhythm. Don't live off beat.

REFLECTION QUESTIONS

Consider these questions and write down your answers in your journal.

1. What is interfering with your rest?
2. What habits do you need to alter so that you can enter into the rhythm of rest for your life?
3. Are you suffering from sleep debt?
4. How will you lower that debt?
5. Are there foods you need to stop eating?
6. Are there foods or drinks that you need to stop eating at a certain time?
7. What are your one day wins for today?

A PRAYER FOR YOU TO PRAY

Father, thank You for caring about all the details in my life. I ask that You continually reveal to me what is interfering with my rest and show me what habits I need to change. Help me to implement what I have learned in this chapter. In Jesus' Name, amen.

CHAPTER 9

REST ACCOMPANIES VICTORY

So the Lord gave to Israel all the land of which He had sworn to give to their fathers, and they took possession of it and dwelt in it. The Lord gave them rest all around, according to all that He had sworn to their fathers. And not a man of all their enemies stood against them; the Lord delivered all their enemies into their hand. Not a word failed of any good thing which the Lord had spoken to the house of Israel. All came to pass.

—Joshua 21:43-45 (NKJV)

In this passage, we see that God gave the Israelites rest after hard-fought battles and victory. They entered a time of prolonged rest. If you are a person who is praying for breakthrough and victory in a certain area of your life, saying, "God, how do I get my breakthrough? How do I get through this battle and fight?"—take a step back. If you take a rest as the Holy Spirit is leading you to and meditate on His Word like we shared, then you'll hear from Him and you'll get the victory. Afterward, you'll enter into a time of a prolonged rest.

Prolonged rest is a season of renewal. In this season that He has planned for you, what do you do in this special time? You build and you prosper.

Asa did what was good and right in the eyes of the Lord his God, for he removed the altars of the foreign gods and the high places, and broke down the sacred pillars and cut down the wooden images. He commanded Judah to seek the Lord God of their fathers, and to observe the law and the commandment. He also removed the high places and the incense altars from all the cities of Judah, and the kingdom was quiet under him. And he built fortified cities in Judah, for the land had rest; he had no war in those years, because the Lord had given him rest. Therefore he said to Judah, "Let us build these cities and make walls around them, and towers, gates, and bars, while the land is yet before us, because we have sought the Lord our God; we have sought Him, and He has given us rest on every side." So they built and prospered.

—2 Chronicles 14:2-7 (NKJV)

When you have prolonged times of rest, it doesn't mean you don't do anything. It's a time for you build, prosper, and grow stronger at a slower pace. In the times of King Asa, the kingdom of Judah had a prolonged period of rest. What did they wisely use that time to do? The Scriptures said they built and prospered. After Saul was converted in the Book of Acts, what did the early church experience? Acts 9:31 (KJV) says, "Then had the churches rest throughout all Judaea and Galilee and Samaria, and were edified; and walking in the fear of the Lord, and in the comfort of the Holy Ghost, were multiplied."

Saul was the chief persecutor and antagonist of the church. His conversion ended a reign of terror for the early Christians. They experienced rest from his attacks because of the great victory the Lord had accomplished. After that victory, the churches had rest, were strengthened, lived in reverence toward God, enjoyed the comforting encouragement of the Holy Spirit, and multiplied and increased.

You might say, "That sounds nice. When might I have this prolonged time of rest and prosperity? When's this breakthrough going to happen for me?"

My question for you is, "What is He telling you to do?"

Get into this rhythm of rest. As you do, you will hear from Him. David inquired of the Lord, heard from Him, and had a breakthrough, and you can get the same breakthrough (2 Samuel 5:17-20).

DAVID'S EXAMPLE

In 2 Samuel 7:1, David experienced a time of rest on every side, just like Joshua and the children of Israel did. What did David do during that time? He set his heart to build a house for God. The Lord told David that his son would build the house. However, in this time of rest we see how God marvelously blessed David and established a special covenant promise with him. The promise was so wonderful to David that he overflowed with thanksgiving:

Who am I, O Sovereign Lord, and what is my family, that you have brought me this far? And now, Sovereign Lord, in addition to everything else, you speak of giving your servant a lasting dynasty! Do you deal with everyone this way, O Sovereign Lord?

What more can I say to you? You know what your servant is really like, Sovereign Lord. Because of your promise and according to your will, you have done all these great things and have made them known to your servant.

How great you are, O Sovereign Lord! There is no one like you. We have never even heard of another God like you! What other nation on earth is like your people Israel? What other nation, O God, have you redeemed from slavery to be your own people? You made a great name for yourself when you redeemed your people from Egypt. You performed awesome miracles and drove out the nations and gods that stood in their way. You made Israel your very own people forever, and you, O Lord, became their God.

And now, O Lord God, I am your servant; do as you have promised concerning me and my family. Confirm it as a promise that will last forever.

—2 Samuel 7:18-25 (NLT)

David's prayer of thanksgiving continued on for even more verses. I want to draw your attention to the fact that he received this wonderful promise of God during a time of prolonged rest. If you are going through a fight right now, there is a wonderful prolonged time of rest and building and strengthening and prosperity and enjoyment on the other side of this battle. In order to get there, you are going to have to rest when the Holy Spirit tells you to.

You will need to take some time to just chill, be still, and relax so that you can hear from God. As you hear, you will be able to recoup your strength so that you can finish this battle and enter into the prolonged time of rest. Your striving is not going to get you there. Your "no days off" mentality is not going to get you there. It will get you into some trouble, but it won't get you into that rest.

When you take time to rest, following the instructions of the Spirit of God, getting into the rhythm of rest that is set by the Holy Spirit Himself, your actions are declaring that you will win the battle you're facing. Remember, your decision to rest is an act of faith.

In obedience to the leading of the Holy Spirit, your rest declares, "Thanks be to God who always leads us in triumph in Christ" and "thanks be to God, who gives us the victory" (2 Corinthians 2:14; 1 Corinthians 15:57 NKJV). Your actions declare, "Because He gives me the victory, I'm going to sleep. Because He gives me the victory, I'm going to take time to sit down and rest." As you rest, He will tell you what to do.

This is an important step for some of the break-throughs you're believing for and the victory that you are seeking. It's important to rest because you are setting yourself up to hear more. When you take time to step away and to rest, you will hear from Him. It's part of the rhythm.

Get into the rhythm of rest for your life. You will enjoy it. It will bless and enrich your life. The rhythm of rest flows from God's love for you. Your rest is a declaration of faith in God who loves you! We walk by faith, we live by faith, and we rest by faith. While you rest, God will fight the battle on your behalf.

REFLECTION QUESTIONS

Consider these questions and write down your answers in your journal.

1. What battle or struggle are you dealing with right now?
2. As you pause and inquire of the Lord, what is He leading you to do?
3. What does victory look like?

4. What will you do during your time of prolonged rest that will follow your victory?

A PRAYER FOR YOU TO PRAY

Father, I thank You that in Christ Jesus You always cause me to triumph. Thank You for always giving me the victory. Because You love me, I am more than a conqueror. I take this time to pause and ask for Your wisdom. How should I handle this challenge in front of me? I receive Your help and Your victory. Thank You! In Jesus' Name, amen.

CHAPTER 10

DON'T LIVE OFF BEAT

There is a rhythm to our rest. Sadly, many of us have been living off beat, and that's why we've been exhausted, that's why we haven't been as healthy as we should be in our bodies, in our minds, in our emotions, in our souls, in our spirits, in our marriages, and in our relationships. We haven't seen the fullness of the promises of God because we've been living off beat and have not been living in the rhythm of rest.

> Let us labour therefore to enter into that rest, lest any man fall after the same example of unbelief.
> —Hebrews 4:11 (KJV)

Let us therefore make every effort to enter that rest [of God, to know and experience it for ourselves], so that no one will fall by following the same example of disobedience [as those who died in the wilderness].

—Hebrews 4:11 (AMP)

So let us do our best to enter that rest. But if we disobey God, as the people of Israel did, we will fall.

—Hebrews 4:11 (NLT)

FOLLOWING THE SHEPHERD'S LEADING

We know that one generation of the Israelites did not enter into the rest of God because of their unbelief. When we look at our lives, we realize that we also have to work to enter into the rest, because it's easy within our culture not to enjoy the rest God has for us. We have to work in order to rest. A part of this work is planning your rest, figuring out how you rest, guarding your rest, and actually resting. In the times when you're not resting, your work is making sure that you're disciplined, operating with self-control, following the plan, walking by faith, and pursuing the vision God has given you so that you can actually take time to rest and enjoy the fruit of your life.

> The Lord is my Shepherd [to feed, guide, and shield me], I shall not lack. He makes me lie down in [fresh, tender] green pastures; He leads me beside the still and restful waters. He refreshes and restores my life (my self); He leads me in the paths of righteousness [uprightness and right standing with Him—not for my earning it, but] for His name's sake.
>
> —Psalm 23:1-3 (AMPC)

The Lord is our Shepherd. What does that job description entail? He's feeding us, He's guiding us, and He's shielding us so that we do not lack. Notice in verse 2 that it says that He makes me to lie down in fresh, tender, green pastures. He leads me beside the still and restful waters. In this passage, we see how the Shepherd is leading His sheep to times of grazing and rest. If the Lord is leading you to times of rest, what should you do? Rest.

For many of us, when the Lord leads us to a time of rest, we decide to work instead. When the Lord leads us to rest, we decide to hustle instead. When the Lord is telling us to rest, we do everything but rest. Why does He lead you to times of rest? Because He's your Good Shepherd. You're going to have to follow the Leader. Remember to take advantage of the opportunities to rest that He brings your way.

You have to listen to the voice of God, not just for the big, deep, super-spiritual things, but even for the natural things. He will tell you to rest. He will tell you to take it easy. At times, He'll even lead you to go take a nap. If He does, do you know what you need to do? You need to go take a nap.

As you acknowledge Him in all your ways, He directs your path. As you check in with Him about your day, your plan, your schedule, He will lead you and guide you into all truth. He will help you get into the rhythm of rest for your life so that you can become creatively productive and even supernaturally productive.

There are times when He will lead you to go to bed early. If you are a "night owl" like me, you still need to follow His leading and go to be early. He may be preparing you for something that you aren't expecting. Without knowing what's ahead, if you make a decision to follow the leading of the Spirit of God, you'll get your rest in and be able to handle whatever shows up in your life.

Don't be distracted from your rest. Don't allow the enemy to steal your rest. Make sure you are practicing good self-control and meekness in your emotions and your thought life. When the Shepherd leads you to rest, make sure you rest. Why does He lead you to rest? He cares for you.

> The Lord will give strength to His people; the Lord will bless His people with peace.
> —Psalm 29:11 (NKJV)

This word *peace* comes from the Hebrew word *shalom*. One of the definitions of *shalom* is "rest." Isn't that amazing? The Lord will give strength to

His people. The Lord will bless His people with rest. Peace and rest are blessings, and the Lord wants to bless you with both! Are you turning away the blessing of God? Are you rejecting the gift of God because you refuse to rest?

PICK UP *HIS* PACE

Now, when we talk about rhythm, life can be fast, and it can be slow. The rhythm can be sped up or it can be slowed down. We all know there are some seasons in our life when we have to do a lot. Those are intense seasons that may be fast paced—times when we just have to get things done. However, that's not supposed to be all the time. There are supposed to be some slow-paced seasons.

God will lead you to a fast-paced season when He expects you to get everything done. He expects you to handle business. He expects you to hustle under the blessing and to work hard under the grace of God. He expects you to do that, because you're called to work.

When that season ends, or that project ends, or that time ends, you'll see that sometimes it's followed by a period of slow-paced activity. It's still working, but it's a slower pace. When that happens, are you taking advantage of that slow pace or are you trying to speed it up? Sometimes, God will lead you at a slow pace, because you need to have that slow pace to recover to get ready for another fast season. Don't speed up what God has told you to slow down. That principle also works in reverse. Don't slow down what God has told you to speed up.

Are you currently in the middle of a fast season, but you're struggling and slowing down because you didn't rest when you were supposed to rest? "I'll just hope and wait and maybe God will bring me an opportunity for rest again." Why couldn't you take full advantage of it at the right time? Did you not recognize the opportunity? Did you refuse to follow the Good Shepherd's leading and rest? If you miss that rest, when the fast season returns, your body, your mind, and your emotions won't be ready because you didn't rest when you were supposed to.

You must get into the rhythm of rest so when the door you have been waiting for opens, you can fully take advantage of it—you can go through it with the strength, the energy, the mental clarity, and the emotional stability you need.

It really is possible. You can work hard under the blessing and get the job done. You can enjoy rest and get into the slower rhythm, and then you pick up the speed again when it's time.

God wants you to be supernaturally and creatively productive and fruitful decade after decade, and for even more decades to come. God doesn't want you to just be a "flash in the pan" or a one-hit wonder. God wants you to flourish throughout all of your life, not just for a short period of your life. In order to do that, you have to get into the rhythm of rest, and that rhythm is set by the Holy Ghost—not you.

Practice the A.I.M. principles. As you listen and follow Him, He'll tell you what to do, whether He uses a still small voice or that peace on the inside. He'll tell you where to go. He'll tell you, "You need to speed it up." He'll tell you, "You need to slow it down." He'll tell you, "You need to take a break." He'll tell you, "You need to go on vacation." He'll tell you, "You need to say yes to this project." He'll tell you, "You need to say no to that project." He'll tell you, "You need to say yes to this opportunity. Yes, you need to go here. You need to do that."

God is always preparing you. Remember, as John 16:13 says, He's showing you things to come. There are times He'll tell you to do things ahead of time so that you're ready when different situations arise in the future. You may not understand, because you don't know all the things that are coming, but when He's telling you to do something, He's preparing you.

Stay in step with the Holy Spirit. As Galatians 5:16 (NKJV) says, "Walk in the Spirit, and you shall not fulfill the lust of the flesh." In the New Living Translation it says, "So I say, let the Holy Spirit guide your lives. Then you won't be doing what your sinful nature craves."

Get into the rhythm of the Spirit; it's the rhythm of rest. Previously in this book, I shared a time when Pastor George Pearsons and I discussed this topic after I ministered on the subject. On that day, he shared a faith confession and affirmation that he says every day. I have adopted it and made it one of my faith confessions and affirmations as well. You should make this something that you say every day as well:

"I have all the time I need to get done everything that I need to get done, with plenty of time left over."

Why should we say that? Many people say the exact opposite. They say, "I don't have enough time in the day. I don't have enough hours in the day." They also continually list all of the things that they can't do.

God has given us all the same 24 hours. To get the most out of our 24 hours, you have to change your mindset and your confession. You have to start continually saying, "I have all the time that I need to get done what I need to get done, with plenty of time left over."

After Pastor George shared that confession, he asked me a question. He said, "You know what I do with that plenty of time left over? I rest."

Don't turn down opportunities to rest when God brings them your way. Get into the rhythm of rest for your life. Peace and rest are blessings, and the Shepherd will lead you to times of rest. Follow the leader and get into the rhythm of rest for your life. Stay in step with the Holy Spirit and don't live off beat.

CHANGE YOUR MINDSET

You need to change the words of your mouth so that you can have that expectation in your life. That's how you become supernaturally efficient, supernaturally effective, and creatively productive. You have all the time that you need to get done what you need to get done with plenty of time left over. What do you do with that plenty of time left over? You rest and keep on enjoying your life.

I strongly believe that God will speak to you in times of rest. You might say, "I've been praying. I've been fasting. I've been studying. I'm just trying to get this answer from God."

What if you just rest? What if you actually follow the leading of the Spirit of God and rest? You'll be amazed at what He tells you when you actually rest. So many people are missing directions from God because they will not rest. Don't let that be you!

I have learned a few different things about listening for His leading. When I take time to rest and go on vacation, for the first few days He will probably talk to me about me. He won't talk to me about ministry or sermon topics until near the end of my time of rest. He'll save the work-related things until the appropriate time so that I can rest first. Do you really think the Spirit of God, who's leading you to rest, doesn't know how you operate and what you need?

When you follow the Shepherd into times of rest, He gives you what you need in your spirit, in your soul, in your mind, in your emotions, in your body, in your finances, in your marriage, and in your family. You have to get into the rhythm of rest so you don't miss the direction of God. Well-meaning, noble-hearted believers are missing revelation from God because they won't rest. My friend, please don't be one of them. Your life would be more enriched if you found out how you rest and got into the rhythm of rest for your life.

The rhythm of rest for your life is set by the Spirit of God. It's not set by your reason. You take everything you know and present it before the Spirit of God and inquire, "How do I apply this in my life? How do I get into the rhythm of rest for my life?" Then you allow the Holy Spirit to set the pace for your life.

Some people say, "Well, I know I need to rest when I'm exhausted." That's not rhythm. If you only rest when you're exhausted, that's not healthy. You're not supposed to be led by exhaustion; you're created to be led by the Spirit (Romans 8:14).

By nature, I'm a person who keeps pushing and pushing through exhaustion until I don't even know how tired I really am. You may be wired like me. We just keep pushing, pushing, pushing. We don't realize how tired we are until we stop and then suddenly need several days to recover. That's not rhythm. I have had to learn not to do this by personally putting into practice what I have taught you in this book.

Learn what you need so you do not hit the proverbial wall of exhaustion. If an object is moving at a high speed and hits a wall, there is always damage. When you hit the wall of forced rest and have to stop, you're out of energy, and now your body, your mind, and your emotions need to recover.

Don't live that way. You have to take regular times of rest. Yes, you need to schedule longer vacations at different times throughout the year. That's good, but you also have to take small breaks. Learn how you're wired and what is going on in your soul and body. You must take time to examine your life and talk to the Spirit of God about it.

You might say, "Well, I don't have the funds to take elaborate vacations."

First, you can get into the rhythm of rest without an elaborate vacation. Second, you can set your faith for God to bring you what you need so that you can take a vacation that you enjoy. God will give you vacations and things just because you enjoy them (1 Timothy 6:17).

Rest is more than just a desire or an enjoyment. It is a need. What does Philippians 4:19 (NLT) tell us? It says, "And this same God who takes care of me will supply all your needs from his glorious riches, which have been given to us in Christ Jesus."

When it comes to your rest, if you don't currently have the funds you need, you can believe God and He'll bring it in. While you wait for it to arrive, you can still rest. You can still get in the rhythm. Don't let the enemy lie to you, saying, "You can't rest because you don't have enough money to rest." Don't agree with him, saying things like, "Rest is for rich people."

Stop saying that. Why? First of all, you *are* rich. Proverbs 10:22 (NLT) says, "The blessing of the Lord makes a person rich, and he adds no sorrow with it." In this rhythm of rest, you'll discover that the Lord's blessing is making you richer every single moment of every single day. It's far more than just money. It's an abundant supply of His goodness in every area of your life.

Learning how to rest will prolong your life and make it more enjoyable, and you'll be a more enjoyable person to be around. You might not be an enjoyable person because you never learned how to rest. When you finally get into the rhythm of rest, that joy and peace of God flows from you and other people enjoy being around you. It'll make your marriage and your family time far richer in quality. It will make your home an enjoyable place to be, and you'll have an enjoyable life because you entered into the rhythm of rest.

Remember, Psalm 46:10 tells us to stop striving, be still, relax, and know that He is God. As I shared time and time again in this book, yes, there are times when you work hard under the blessing and grace of God. However, sometimes we work past the Spirit's leading because we're not in a place of faith. We strive and toil because we don't believe God can handle it.

FAITH VS. UNBELIEF

When the Spirit of God tells you to go rest or take the day off, don't say, "No, I have to do this, I have to do this. Everything's going to crumble if I don't do this." The Spirit of God is telling you to stop. But you say, "I have to."

That is a sign of unbelief. It's a sign of fear. It's a sign that you don't realize that God is God. The rhythm of rest for our life flows from faith, discipline, self-control, having a vision, and working the plan. That's how you stay in the rhythm of rest for your life. It's how you handle anxiety. It's how you can tackle worry and defeat fear. Rest is a place where revelation will flow. There is so much more that He wants to share with you. In order to experience His revelations, you have to enter into the rhythm of rest for your life.

Have you ever noticed that there are times when you wake up in the morning, before you're fully get going, that you hear God talk to you about things? Or when you have dreams and visions during the night, God's talking to you about things. Why? You're in a place of rest. How much more revelation would you receive if you got into the rhythm of rest for your life? It's the rhythm set by the Spirit of God. You'll be working with Him and partnering with

Him. You'll become even more effective in His king-dom and in accomplishing His plan for your life.

Remember, you can be working in your calling, doing wonderful things, doing what is good, but still be toiling. You could be doing the right things, just off beat. That is where we get tricked. We think, "I'm doing what's right. Why isn't my body feeling better? I'm doing what I'm called to do."

The question isn't whether you are doing what God called you to do, but are you resting? When God called you, He planned times of rest for you. You can be doing the right thing and still end up in a time of forced rest because you did not rest when He told you to.

As I train other ministers, they might say, "I got up to preach and the anointing was there." That's their reason for overworking.

I reply, "Of course it was—you're anointed." That's their gift, which God has deposited in them for life.

They'll say, "Well, God moved." That's why they continued going long after they were supposed to stop.

My reply? "Of course He did—the Word's anointed."When we encounter God's Word, it should be normal for us to encounter the God of the Word as well.

But was it work or toil?

Here is what I ask next:"What happened after the anointing lifted and the service was over? How was your physical, emotional, and mental health? Was it good or was it jacked up?"

If your overall health is a complete mess, how can that be because you are anointed and in the service of God? What kind of witness is that? We don't serve a God who uses up His ministers until they're burned out and wrecked! That's not our Good Shepherd!

If your health is in bad shape, it's because you're not resting. A wonderful move of God does not mean you can't take time to rest. When I study wonderful moves of God in the past and the revivalists who led them, some of their ministries ended early because they did not take care of their bodies. They did not rest and they ate horribly. You are not excused from rest just because you're anointed and are active in an effective ministry.

SUPERNATURAL REST LEADS TO CREATIVITY

We have covered how not resting can come from a lack of faith. We also talked about how it can happen when you lack a plan. As I'm sure you have heard before, if you fail to plan, you plan to fail. If you don't plan to rest, guess what? You're not going to rest. You have to be disciplined so that you can work your plan. Develop a vision for what your rest will look like. Vision produces endurance and self-control, and it's going to help you rest and enjoy the fruit of your labor.

Psalm 46:10 in the Amplified Bible, Classic Edition says, "Let be and be still, and know (recognize and understand) that I am God. I will be exalted among the nations! I will be exalted in the earth!"

There's something so wonderful and supernatural about resting and knowing that He is God. There's so much to encounter and learn while you rest. Remember, when you make a decision to rest and get into the rhythm of rest for your life, you are making a powerful declaration of your faith in God and your belief in His blessing. By your actions, you are declaring that God can cause you to become supernaturally creative and productive as you rest. You are announcing that God will take care of things for you as you rest. As you get back into working, because work is part of the rhythm of rest, you'll be able to say, "I've rested, so now I'm going to work under the blessing. Now I'm going to be supernaturally creative."

God has more for you. Get into the rhythm of rest. It's time for you to live in a new, higher, and better way. The way you experience rest may change as you age and mature. The rest you need today may not be how you rested five years ago or what you may need ten years from now. However, when you live in the rhythm of rest, you will be able to make the necessary adjustments as time goes by.

A striving and toiling mentality says, "Nothing will ever change. The only way I can prosper, the only way I can make a living, the only way I'll go forward is if I rarely stop, if I push through the exhaustion, if I never take off days, and if I grind until I drop." If you do that, you'll be stunted in your progress because part of the rhythm of rest is being creative. When you are creative, you are letting your faith combine with your imagination as you look for opportunities to rest.

As we have already covered, Proverbs 10:22 tells us that the blessing of the Lord makes a person rich without painful toil. The Lord has a way for you to increase without painful toil. Yes, He expects you to work hard and smart under the blessing but not in painful toil doing things your way. Don't mistake *activity* for *productivity*.

Stop limiting yourself to what the world does and the way they strive and toil to achieve success. You have a wonderful covenant with God. Creativity is necessary when it comes to experiencing the rest God has for you and living in the rhythm. With the things that are currently happening in the earth and the things that are coming that will further upset the status quo, you will need to learn how to actually rest in the midst of it all.

You can't say, "Well, I'll only be able to rest if this happens in the economy and this happens in the nation." What happens if it doesn't happen? Will you refuse to rest?

Stop letting your rest be determined by what goes on in the world. In order to do that, you are going to have to expand the way you think. Step outside of what you've experienced. Pastor David Crank once said, "A mind expanded never returns to its original condition."

Think about all of the changes that happened in our world in 2020. It was a tumultuous year of change. However, the people who were the most adaptable in 2020 prospered. The people who were stuck in their ways fell behind. Now, I'm not saying what happened 2020 is going to happen again, but what if something global happens and you need to shift again? Will you give up on the rhythm of rest? Will you still hold to your old model, or are you willing to innovate? Are you willing to change? The rhythm of rest will help you pivot, because the rhythm of rest is set by the Holy Ghost. Remember,

I'm not telling you create your own rest or your own rhythm. No, you're staying in the rhythm and the flow of the Holy Spirit. In this rhythm, you learn to become flexible and to remain open to the leading of the Spirit.

REFLECTION QUESTIONS

Consider these questions and write down your answers in your journal.

1. Are you living off beat?
2. What does a fast-paced season look like to you?
3. What does a slow-paced season look like to you?
4. In reflecting over your life, have you been ignoring your Shepherd's leadings to rest?
5. Do you have to change your mentality where rest is concerned? If so, where?
6. What causes you to be distracted from taking times of rest?
7. What are your one day wins for today?
8. How will you implement what you learned in this chapter?

A PRAYER FOR YOU TO PRAY

Father, thank You for loving me so much that You desire to bless me with peace and rest. Thank You for being my Good Shepherd. I desire to yield to Your leading. Help me to implement what I learned in this chapter. In Jesus' Name, amen.

CONCLUSION

∿

As I write the conclusion of this book, I am reminded of the blueprints of the tabernacle and temple in the Old Testament. God gave Moses the blueprint for building the tabernacle. Similarly, God gave David the blueprint for the Temple, and David left those instructions for Solomon. I believe the rhythm of rest is God's blueprint that shows you how to build and enjoy a fulfilling and impactful life. As I write these words, I am imagining Him sitting next to you handing you a scrolled blueprint. You can take the blueprint by enacting the principles of the rhythm of rest.

As you implement the principles of this book, I know that your quality of life will continue to improve. The rhythm of rest is a higher way for you to live. Don't be discouraged if you get off beat from time to time. Definitely do not quit! When you notice you are off beat, get back into the rhythm. As you continue to live in the rhythm of rest, you will learn more, grow in understanding, and enjoy the life God has for you.

Finishing this book is a one day win for me. There have been several one day wins over a period of months that have led me to this moment. After I pen the next several sentences, I plan to go and celebrate my one day win with my family. Why? I do my best to live by the principles of this book and I encourage you to do the same.

God has a great plan for your life. As you live in the rhythm of rest, you will fulfill that plan and experience a life overflowing with the goodness and joy of God. Your life will radiate His goodness, causing others to want to know Him. God has a rhythm of rest for you because He loves you. Respond to His love today by entering into the rhythm of rest for your life.

MY PRAYER FOR YOU

Father, I pray for all of those reading this book and those who are listening to it being read to them. I pray that You help them enter the rhythm of rest for their life. Rest was Your original plan for us. It is still Your plan for us. Help us to take advantage of the opportunities of rest You bring our way. As a result, I pray that You will cause us to become supernaturally creative, innovative, and efficient. I pray that You will cause each reader and listener to thrive, progress, and prosper spiritually, emotionally, mentally, physically, socially, and financially. I know how much You love them! Help them to grow in awareness and in understanding of Your love. Grant them the blessings of peace and rest. Keep them safe and deliver them from all the attacks of the wicked one. Thank You for the opportunity to pour into their lives through this book. In Jesus' Name, amen.

ENDNOTES

1 Dzifa Adjaye-Gbewonyo, Amanda E. Ng, Lindsey I. Black, "Sleep Difficulties in Adults: United States, 2020," CDC.gov, NCHS Data Brief No. 436, June 2022, https://www.cdc.gov/nchs/products/databriefs/db436.htm.

2 "What Are Sleep Deprivation and Deficiency?" National Heart, Lung, and Blood Institute, March 24, 2022, https://www.nhlbi.nih.gov/health/sleep-deprivation.

3 Ibid.

4 RAND Press Release, "Lack of Sleep Costing U.S. Economy Up to $411 Billion a Year," Rand.org, November 30, 2016, https://www.rand.org/news/press/2016/11/30.html.

5   Ibid.

6   Rebecca Zucker, "How Taking a Vacation Improves Your Well-Being," Harvard Business Review, July 19, 2023, https://hbr.org/2023/07/how-taking-a-vacation-improves-your-well-being.

7   Pavilion University HQ, "The Real Cost of Burnout—On Your People and Your Bottom Line," Pavilion University Blog, May 4, 2022, https://www.joinpavilion.com/blog/the-real-cost-of-burnout.

8   "How Much Sleep Is Enough," National Heart, Lung, and Blood Institute, March 24, 2022, https://www.nhlbi.nih.gov/health/sleep-deprivation/how-much-sleep.

9   KidsHealth Medical Experts, "Does the Light From a Screen Make it Hard to Sleep?" Kids Health.org, accessed April 24, 2025, https://kids health.org/en/teens/blue-light.html.

10 Matthew Solan, "Eating junk food may affect deep sleep," Harvard Health, September 1, 2023, https://www.health.harvard.edu/staying-healthy/eating-junk-food-may-affect-deep-sleep.

ABOUT KERRICK BUTLER

Kerrick A.R. Butler II is an author, broadcaster, civic leader, and pastor. Kerrick serves as senior pastor of Faith Christian Center located in Mableton, Georgia. He is a graduate of Word of Faith Bible Training Center and Oral Roberts University. Kerrick believes wholeheartedly in sharing the message of Jesus through creative avenues to help people apply Bible truths to their everyday lives. Kerrick, his wife, Racquel, and their beautiful family reside in Metro Atlanta.

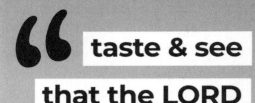

**taste & see
that the LORD**
is good
blessed are those
who trust in **Him!**

PSALM 33:8

Start your weekdays
with faith and
encouragement by
streaming

PASTOR KERRICK'S

FAITH IN THE
MORNING

**podcast
devotional**